Brain

on

Fire

Confronting the burning
issues of today . . . and
tomorrow

Lawrence C. Marsh

Brain on Fire
Confronting the burning issues of today
. . . and tomorrow.

Emeritus Publishing
P.O. Box 480852
Kansas City, Missouri 64148
http://emerituspublishing.com
info@emerituspublishing.com

Copyright by Lawrence C. Marsh
First Paperback Edition 2011
Printed in the United States of America.

ISBN-978-0-9828521-9-4 (paperback)
Library of Congress LCCN/ PCN: 2011924361

Marsh, Lawrence C.
Brain on Fire: confronting the burning issues of today
• • • and tomorrow.

Includes 237 references and 706 indexed words/phrases.

Commentary on economics, energy, education, health, foreign affairs, politics, future world and related topics.

QUICK SUMMARY OF CONTENTS

1. Energy Policy: 21
   price floors, tariffs and trade

2. 21st Century Challenges: 39
   technology and climate change

3. Education: 55
   confronting old issues and new
   developments

4. Economic Theory: 71
   new challenges to an old paradigm

5. Economic Policy: 93
   money, taxes and minimum wage

6. Research Methods: 105
   system dynamics forecasting and
   problems with randomized trials

7. Foreign Affairs: 119
   Africa, foreign aid and China

8. Terrorism and the Middle East:　135
   Iran, Israel, profiling and no-fly

9. Afghanistan:　147
   elections, stability and U.S. troops

10. Attitudes and Beliefs:　157
    underlying behavioral motivation
    and incentives

11. Health Policy:　171
    health insurance, fee-for-service,
    fat-taxes, doctors and dentists

12. Personal Health:　189
    weight loss and weak bones

13. Future World:　211
    DNA, nanotechnology, ocean living,
    Internet advertising and shopping

TABLE OF CONTENTS

Introduction   15

1. Energy Policy: 21
   price floors, tariffs and trade

   Gulf oil spill disaster: Collective risk requires
       collaborative risk management   22

   Define "energy independence" in terms of
       both oil price and quantity   24

   Curb petro-dictators and promote green jobs
       with a price floor on crude oil imports   26

   Carbon tax better than trying to pick
       alternative energy winner   32

   An energy plan for Congress: A dynamic, self-
       adjusting price floor for gasoline   34

   Law professors propose new gasoline tax
       with categorical rebates   37

2. 21st Century Challenges: 39
   technology, immigration,
   newspapers and climate change

H-1B visas, highly-skilled immigrants and
   our knowledge economy   41

Techno-nationalists may hurt, not help America 43

How the poor exploit the rich   44

Aliens have taken over Planet Earth   46

Four myths about newspapers
   and online advertising   48

Revealed preference "Daily Me" key
   to online newspaper survival   51

Is there more to our climate problems than
   just global warming   53

3. Education: 55
   confronting old issues and new
   developments

Flynn Effect, IQ scores and SAT scores:
   Are our children smarter than we are?   56

Google Books changes everything in student
   teacher education   60

Spend some of those millions for educational
    video games   63

New math can succeed with right attitude
    and priorities   66

Espresso Book Machine offers hot book
    with your coffee   68

Obama honorary degree consistent with
    Notre Dame traditions   69

4. Economic Theory: 71
new challenges to old paradigm

Job losses may be permanent   72

Restoring the efficiency of free markets   73

Paul Samuelson played a key role in the
    foundation of modern economics   75

Ostrom and Williamson win Nobel Prize   77

Economic theory must change to accommodate
    irrational, inconsistent, altruistic behavior   79

The next frontier in economics:
    Creating markets for mental energy   85

Does "Creative Capitalism" as proposed
    by Bill Gates make sense?   87

Are you a socialist-creationist or a
    free-market evolutionist?   90

5. Economic Policy: 93
money, taxes and minimum wage

Should California be allowed to create
    its own money?   95

Without taxes money would have no value   97

Bernanke versus Geithner:
    their roles for credit or blame   98

Enhance financial security, cut income taxes
    with tax-deferred savings plan   101

Conservatives and liberals oversimplify
    analysis of minimum wage   103

6. Research Methods: 105
system dynamics forecasting and
problems with randomized trials

Research needed to end economy's
    boom-bust cycle   107

Problems in business and economic analysis   110

System dynamics is key to success in
    economic forecasting   112

Control variables needed in randomized trials   115

7. Foreign Affairs: 119
Africa, foreign aid and China

Has 50 years of U.S. AID money stymied
    African growth?   121

Can free markets and local businesses convert
    poverty into prosperity when foreign aid fails? 124

To promote capitalism and enhance
    our soft power, go to Kiva.org   127

Freedom and democracy in China   129

Cheap Chinese tires challenge Obama
    trade strategy   131

8. Terrorism and the Middle East: 135
Iran, Israel, profiling and no-fly

Can profiling stop terrorists?   136

Make 90-day no-fly the default for terrorists   137

Psychiatrist Nidal Malik Hasan programmed
  himself for murder   139

Strange strategy backfires: Iranian President
  Ahmadinejad fools no one except himself   141

Obama drops missile shield to end cold war
  strategy   142

Netanyahu reverses peace prosperity logic   144

9. Afghanistan: 147
elections, stability and U.S. troops

Afghan election fraud hard pill to swallow   148

Afghanistan mirrors Chechnya, not Vietnam   149

How to determine if we can achieve stability
  in Iraq and Afghanistan   151

Obama's Afghan "Human Terrain" strategy   153

10. Attitudes and Beliefs: 157
underlying behavioral motivation
and incentives

Darwin, race and racial attitudes in America   158

Martin Luther King, Jr. saved America 161

Sergeant Crowley versus Harvard's Professor
  Henry Louis Gates, Jr. 162

Driving-while-texting (DWT) more dangerous
  than driving-under-the-influence (DUI) 164

Seat belt choice: protect people or your car? 165

Some Wall Street greed can never be satisfied 166

What do trademarks and brand names protect? 169

11. Health Policy: 171
health insurance, fee-for-service, fat-taxes, doctors and dentists

Medical research fails to deliver personal prognosis 173

The incentive structure of our health care system
  is all wrong 175

Make people pay extra for their bad health habits 178

To some libertarians even private health
  insurance is a bad idea 180

Will public option health insurance doom us to
  a life of socialism? 182

Obama failed to fully address the perverse
   fee-for-service incentive system   185

Asymmetric information leads to market failure
   in dentistry   186

12. Personal Health: 189
weight loss and weak bones

No-Eat-Day Diet: A good strategy or bad advice? 190

Is calorie restriction a good defense against
   cancer?   191

Reprogram your subconscious mind to commit
   terrorism or lose weight   193

Why healthy living didn't protect
   Bill Clinton's heart   196

Men in their 70s must be defensive players   198

Bone density and osteoporosis   200

Why cavemen didn't have weak bones   203

Should you be required to see
   a doctor once a year?   204

Irrational behavior exposes flaw in
   economic theory   207

13. Future World: 211
DNA, nanotechnology, ocean living, Internet advertising and shopping

Stores like Wal-Mart need shopping list
    reminder boxes   213

Make money just by wearing an electronic
    "Ink" t-shirt   214

Forget Mars, there's plenty of land under
    our oceans   216

Stem cells and nanosurgery may change
    what it means to be human   218

Three rules for dealing with backup copies
    of your brain   220

Altering animal DNA:
    Would you like your dog to talk?   222

If your friends don't answer their cell phones
    just give them a nanonudge   224

References   226

Index   238

Acknowledgements   249

About the Author   250

Introduction

A rchaeologists have identified a period of relative climate stability since the last ice age as a key factor allowing humanity to escape the day-to-day struggle for survival. This break in climatic volatility enabled humanity to evolve rapidly in recent millennia. Millions of years of a daily struggle for survival have been replaced by relative prosperity in many parts of the world. Today we face less dramatic but important challenges to stability: (1) volatility in income and consumption in the form of economic booms and busts, (2) terrorism and political volatility in some parts of the world, (3) volatility in fossil fuel prices, and, once again, (4) some degree of volatility in climate.

Brain on Fire addresses all of these forms of volatility by proposing a progressive consumption tax to replace our current progressive income tax, more effective ways of dealing with terrorism and world disorder, a price floor for foreign crude oil imports as well as a dynamic, self-adjusting price floor for gasoline, and increased attention to the advent of abrupt changes in climate beyond just global warming.

Volatility is just one of the challenges we face. Another important challenge is the degeneration of our democracy into incessant, partisan bickering. American political thought has become locked in a one-dimensional framework. We find ourselves trapped in a single left-right spectrum ranging from liberal to conservative. There are a myriad of other ways of looking at the world for both domestic and foreign policy analysis, but we can't seem to get out of the left-right trap. Partisan bickering smothers just about every policy proposal advanced.

Common ground does not seem to exist. Our political life has degenerated into a sort of bipolar disorder switching between conservative and liberal.

Brain on Fire initiates new ideas offering new dimensions. Economics provides the important dimension of incentives. From a big picture point of view, the incentive dimension tends to favor conservatives. After all, Adam Smith understood the importance of incentives, but Karl Marx did not.

On the other hand, free enterprise cannot always guarantee optimal incentives. Liberals can sometimes find their side benefiting from the incentive perspective. It is the perverse nature of the fee-for-service system for paying doctors that has driven up health care costs. Patients often don't know and don't care about costs as long as insurance is paying. Consequently, doctors and patients have no incentive to hold down health care costs.

The financial system meltdown was due to the failure of incentives as well. The desire for bigger bonuses in the short run drove some mortgage bankers to forego prudent, long-term precautions and make untenable home loans. Free enterprise incentives failed us again.

Incentives also reach into the school room where our children too often find themselves uninspired at best or bored at worst. Kids who compete ferociously at video games can exhibit little or no incentive in their education.

Ignoring incentives to pursue a left-wing or right-wing agenda does not lead to formulating the best possible policies or to establishing the common ground needed to enact them. Getting incentive right is a key theme in this book.

Matching costs to benefits through taxes and subsidies is another theme throughout the book. It provides another dimension of analysis for evaluating

INTRODUCTION

proposed policies. As children we are told to pick up after ourselves and clean up our rooms. We can't expect others to carry our costs.

Companies and individuals that generate costs for society as a whole or other individuals or companies must be held accountable for those costs. Businesses that dump pollutants into a river must pay for the economic loss to those downstream who rely on clean water from that river. This sometimes means assessing the value of such external costs and assigning it through taxation or other mechanisms to the individuals, companies or even entire industries that generate them. Unassigned external costs are known to economists as *negative externalities*. Negative externalities lead to a form of market failure where resources are wasted because private costs don't include all the relevant costs of an activity.

Common property resource systems such as shared fishing grounds, clean water and clean air can generate destructive behavior as each player tries to exploit the resource for short-term gain. Private property ownership, or extractive operations that take the full cost of using these resources into account, will more likely produce optimal, as opposed to excessive, usage. There is an optimal level of pollution, but our current system produces pollution that is well above the optimal level. Private costs must incorporate the full cost to society of exploiting resources to attain the optimal cost-benefit solution within a free-enterprise system.

The opposite can occur when individuals or companies generate *positive externalities* that inadvertently help others. When government or citizens as a whole benefit from such activities, it makes sense to provide an appropriate subsidy. For example, subsidies can encourage flu vaccination or the purchase of energy-efficient automobiles or appliances.

Our economy allocates resources more efficiently when costs are matched more precisely to benefits. The household runs more efficiently when every child cleans up his or her own room.

Empowerment is another dimension examined in *Brain on Fire*. As individuals obtain greater wealth, they desire and demand more control over their lives as well as more meaning and accomplishment in their work. Finding an outlet for their creativity and their desire to seek a greater purpose is more important than ever. Treating people as sheep who just need food, shelter and a little guidance doesn't cut it. We must resist policies that take away people's control and promote policies that empower people to take charge of their own lives.

Some argue that conservative social policies restrict individual rights, while liberal economic policies do the same from the left. The empowerment dimension recognizes our shared interdependence while going beyond freedom to autonomy. Freedom means not allowing others to control our lives. Freedom alone is like a car speeding down the highway with no one at the wheel. Liberals translate the conservative philosophy of "free to choose" into "free to lose." Empowerment implies autonomy where we gain control of our own lives. Autonomy puts us in the driver's seat.

Sometimes entire countries are motivated by a need for autonomy and empowerment when they have a history of subjugation. In particular, understanding China requires an understanding of Chinese history and the subjugation of China initially by European powers and later by Japan. In the United States we have not experienced foreign domination since our creation as a nation. History is replete with examples of countries willing to sacrifice internal freedom to better guarantee their external freedom. Even in the United States we allowed more government wiretapping in response to 9/11. China's history of internal volatility has added to its concern for stability in addition to autonomy. These factors play an important role in China's insistence on selling its products at low, discount prices to the rest of the world in order to maintain adequate levels of employment in China. An unstable China is in no one's interest, but at the same time all countries must avoid excessive manipulation of foreign currency markets.

In addition to challenging the conventional wisdom in economics, we must also address similar problems in medicine. Unlike physics and economics, medicine has little or no theory and is almost entirely empirically based. Little work has been done to explain how the body's electrical system interfaces with its chemical system or how the digestive system and circulatory system interact. Medical theories must be developed that provide us with a better understanding of how our bodies work to guide us in improving health and extending life.

The traditional one-size-fits-all approach to applying information from medical research studies to individual patients must be changed to incorporate the data from individual patients back into the equations. This is now at last becoming feasible with the digitization of patient records.

Recent research suggests a need for new medical strategies and procedures. The traditional cholesterol theory for explaining heart attacks and strokes may need to give way to the homocysteine theory that takes into account the damage done to artery walls by transfats and partially hydrogenated oils. C-reactive protein may also play a key role along with excessive physical and psychological stress.

Osteoporosis research must go beyond the study of bone density and also consider the cellular matrix structure provided by cell proteins. Drugs that merely block the normal cycle of replacing old bone with new bone are not optimal. New drugs that enhance cytocine-10 production for the formation of new bone are needed. Drugs should enhance, not block, the bone replacement cycle. Weight bearing exercise and low-acid eating are key to enhancing bone strength.

The last section, called *Future World*, provides insight into problems arising from advances in stem cells, nanotechnology and DNA research, which all promise great benefits if handled well, but may pose serious problems if we don't give these issues sufficient forethought. Anticipating the future is the first step in preparing properly for it.

To make real progress in a world that is rapidly changing we must break out of the old, one-dimensional way to thinking and explore new concepts and alternative approaches that offer better solutions through multi-dimensional analysis. *Brain on Fire* is an attempt to begin this process.

1. Energy Policy:
price floors, tariffs and trade

World energy markets are highly integrated. Isolating ourselves from the rest of the world is neither desirable nor realistic. This chapter discusses our collective energy interdependence and some strategies for freeing ourselves from foreign oil dependency without isolating us from the world.

A key aspect of energy independence involves preventing sudden, dramatic dips in the price of oil from wiping out alternative energy investments. Whenever fossil fuel prices fall significantly, alternative energy companies soon lose many of their customers. As soon as an alternative energy company begins to miss payments, creditors and their lawyers quickly force the company into bankruptcy before more assets are drained away. In 2008 a number of alternative energy firms went bankrupt when gasoline prices fell from just over $4 a gallon to around $1.60 a gallon.

When economists analyze long-term trends they often use moving averages that smooth over abrupt dips and spikes in prices. Import tariffs and domestic taxes can be used in an analogous manner to smooth energy prices to counteract energy price volatility. Variable tariffs on crude oil imports and variable taxes on gasoline can be set to disappear when prices are high but fill in to keep prices from sagging below acceptable levels when prices dip in the short run. This prevents short-term market volatility from destroying the long-term viability of alternative energy investments.

Gulf oil spill disaster: Collective risk requires collaborative risk management

What have we learned from seeing oil pour out of BP's wellhead day after day in the Gulf of Mexico? Is it all about fail-safe systems and blow-out preventers?

Who needs to learn a lesson here? It was BP's project, Transoceans' drilling rig and Haliburton's expert advice. Should federal inspectors in general and the Minerals Management Service in particular have done more to prevent this disaster? What about President Obama and our politicians? Shouldn't they be held responsible for not preventing this type of problem? What about the United Nations and the countries that attended the 2009 U.N. climate change summit in Copenhagen?

The reality is that no one is in charge on Planet Earth. We are all collectively responsible for what goes on here. We sometimes like to think of ourselves as independent, rugged individualists epitomized by the "Marlboro Man." An alien intelligence from elsewhere in the universe may not see it that way at all. Instead, humanity may be viewed as a creature made up of cells called "humans" that has spread itself over the land surfaces of the planet. Recognizing our interdependence may ultimately be critical to our collective survival.

Commentator David Brooks noted the similarity of the Three Mile Island disaster, the Challenger disaster, the recent financial disaster and the Gulf of Mexico oil spill disaster. In each case a complex system failed because people in a position to prevent it didn't see it coming or had an incentive to discount the risk. Systems have become too complex and internal pressure to cut costs has become too great for a handful of specialized engineers within a for-profit enterprise to manage safely.

(1.) ENERGY POLICY

Collective risk requires a system of collaborative risk management. Linux, Wikipedia and the Netflix competition show the way. Linux provides a framework for volunteer programmers to work together effectively. Wikipedia does the same in defining and understanding our world. The Netflix competition demonstrated how specialists from around the world can focus on a specific goal and work in teams to solve a complex problem.

To draw on the collective wisdom of specialists who have no profit motive to discount risks, Congress should set up and oversee a national risk management award system by passing the following two-part legislation.

(1) All complex, unclassified systems that could greatly affect the well-being of the public or put substantial public money at risk shall be open systems. Except where national security requires secrecy, the details of such public and private complex systems shall be made available for public scrutiny.

(2) Congress shall oversee an award system providing significant monetary incentives in an annual competition to identify and offer effective solutions for potential disasters. A panel of scientists and engineers would create a system to nominate entries for the annual Congressional awards.

In most areas of private endeavor, we should continue to protect privacy and freedom without government interference. Our patent system already provides a means to protect the innovative ideas of individuals and companies while revealing details of their proprietary systems. Individual freedom is very important, but so is our collective well-being. Finding the right balance between unfettered freedom and proper oversight may well determine the outcome of building the ever more complex systems that enhance our power but also add to our collective vulnerability.

Define "energy independence" in terms of both oil price and quantity

The world oil market is like a giant tank of oil. Canada and Mexico are just two spigots. Our national security does not depend on which spigots we're using, but on the quantity of oil we require and the price we have to pay.

Oil is fungible. It's essentially the same stuff no matter its source. It doesn't matter whether the spigots we use are friendly or unfriendly. It's basically the same oil either way.

Let's say that all the oil entering the United States came from our friends in Canada and Mexico. Would that make us safer? What would happen if some OPEC countries were suddenly to stop supplying oil to the world market?

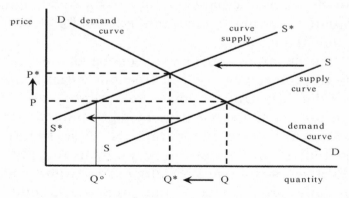

Figure 1. OPEC cuts back supply and price rises

24

(1.) ENERGY POLICY

Figure 1 shows what happens when oil supplies are reduced, shifting the oil supply curve from S to S*. At price P, the quantity supplied would drop initially from Q, first to Q^o, but then price would begin to rise.

In response, other suppliers of oil would try to pump extra oil until supply and demand were in equilibrium once again, but at the higher price P* and new equilibrium quantity Q*.

Oil would still be available, but just at a much higher price. The quantity demanded in world markets would drop somewhat in response to that higher price.

Would non-OPEC countries such as Canada and Mexico keep their prices low to accommodate their good friend the United States? How would they justify that to their citizens? Are they going to be willing to forfeit some of their money so that we can keep more of ours?

If we really want "energy independence," we need to bring the price of oil down by reducing our demand for it. The real problem is that we are currently pouring money into the coffers of petro-dictatorships around the world by purchasing large quantities of oil at high prices. Finding economically viable alternatives to oil can help us shift our demand curve D for oil in Figure 1 downward and leftward to reduce both the price we pay and the quantity we use.

Of course, energy independence involves more than just securing fuel for vehicles. A nation must also consider sources of fuel for generating electricity and any additional sources for heating/cooling and direct power applications, such as in manufacturing.

National security is served best by coming up with homegrown alternative sources of energy such as nuclear, solar, wind and new (as yet unknown) sources of energy while greatly improving our energy efficiency.

France is now getting almost 80 per cent of its electricity from nuclear power.[1] Brazil has virtually all of its vehicles running on E85, which means that 85 per cent of its fuel is ethanol produced from sugar cane.[2] Denmark has recently become energy independent in electricity by investing heavily in wind power.[3]

In the United States we get most of our power for uses other than transportation from domestic sources, with the significant exception of natural gas from Canada. Consequently, for us the issue of energy independence centers on our importation of large quantities of crude oil. We need to develop alternatives so we can buy less oil at lower prices.

Ultimately, for the United States in the long-run buying less foreign oil at lower prices is what energy independence really means. Although we want lower oil prices in the long run, we may have to prevent short-term dips in oil prices from wiping out our alternative energy investments. Keeping oil prices from dropping too abruptly is key to driving them down permanently. This special problem is discussed in the next section.

Curb petro-dictators and promote green jobs with a price floor on crude oil imports

Our national security requires that we reduce our demand for foreign oil and drive down world oil prices. Too much of our oil money is ending up in the hands of anti-American actors. The volatility of crude oil prices will undermine President Obama's efforts to promote green jobs. The energy policies of past administrations failed because they failed to address this volatility.

(1.) ENERGY POLICY

Cheap oil makes alternative energy relatively expensive. It takes only a few months of defaults on interest payments before lawyers for creditors force alternative energy companies into bankruptcy. In the sell-off of assets, billions of dollars of alternative energy investments go right down the drain.

For example, after investing a billion dollars in alternative energy, VeraSun Energy had to declare bankruptcy because of cyclically low oil prices.[4] Standard Oil, under John D. Rockefeller, would occasionally set prices of petroleum products below cost to drive out competitors.[5] The Soviet Union collapsed when a dramatic drop in oil prices undercut the Kremlin's financial viability in the early 1990s.

Since the United States is the greatest consumer of oil in the world, demand for oil within the United States has a major impact on world oil prices. Anything that can be done to reduce the demand for oil in the United States will cause world oil prices to drop.

Consider what happens when a financial crisis occurs somewhere in the world. We have seen such financial crises occur in Asia, Russia, Mexico and other places. Before the crisis, the world price for oil might be around $100 a barrel. The financial crisis causes a sharp reduction in the demand for oil. The drop in demand causes a dramatic reduction in world oil prices to, say, $70 a barrel. The relatively low price for oil quickly bankrupts alternative energy investments that cannot compete when oil prices are unusually low.

How could we use a variable tariff to protect our alternative energy investments in that circumstance? How could such a tariff not only protect alternative energy projects, but also reduce both our demand for oil as well as the world price for oil and, thereby, reduce oil money going to terrorists?

Ordinarily, most economists favor free trade and are, therefore, opposed to tariffs on principle. The areas of energy and environmental economics provide exceptions to this general rule. National security plays a key role.

To ensure the viability of alternative energy, the price of crude oil must be kept high enough within the United States to give reasonable alternative energy projects a chance. Originally at $100 a barrel, the price of oil needs to be kept above a price floor of $80 a barrel to protect alternative energy investments. A price of $70 a barrel is too low and needs to be raised back up to at least $80 a barrel. However, we want the price obtained by anti-American countries and terrorists to be as low as possible.

The answer to this dilemma is to impose a variable tariff on imported crude oil to bring the price of oil within the United States back up to the $80 price floor while forcing world oil prices down. All revenues from the tariff would be given back to American families in the form of a tax rebate.

The variable tariff raises the oil price from $70 to $80 within the United States which depresses demand further and brings the world oil price down to, say, $60. This drives a wedge between the world oil price at $60 and our domestic price for oil at $80 with the tariff taking up the difference of $20. We will have reduced our demand for foreign oil and increased our supply of domestically produced oil. Until and unless we are able to satisfy all of our demand for oil domestically, the variable tariff will bring the price for oil within the United States up to the specified price floor while forcing the world oil price down.

(1.) ENERGY POLICY

This would take money out of the hands of foreign oil producers and into the hands of American families to spend any way they wished. Higher petroleum prices would absorb some of that money, but it would make all other prices relatively cheaper. The substitution effect of higher petroleum prices decreases the demand for oil and shifts that demand to other products. The tax rebate would compensate for the income effect on American families of that oil price increase. By altering relative prices, the net effect would be to lower our overall demand for oil and reduce our dependency on foreign oil.

Over 80 percent of the world's proven oil reserves are owned by foreign governments, some of whom are hostile to the United States. Whenever world oil prices fall to $70 a barrel, a variable tariff on crude oil imports set to maintain a price floor of $80 a barrel could force world oil prices down to around $60 a barrel and deprive Iran, Venezuela, Russia and Saudi Arabia of oil revenues while helping our own energy companies by putting our oil dollars to work right here at home. We are continuing to undermine our own national security and that of our allies such as Israel by sending enormous amounts of oil money overseas to Iran and other sponsors of terrorism.

Ironically, setting a $80 a barrel price floor will tend to keep the price of oil from rising above $80 by keeping alternative energy viable during temporary oil price drops and thus allowing long-term investments in alternative energy. Eliminating the up and down roller coaster in oil prices will improve efficiency and productivity by finally allowing consumers, producers and investors to plan ahead.

The variable tariff would also give our alternative energy companies a comparative advantage over foreign alternative energy companies since our alternative energy

29

companies would benefit from a higher domestic price for oil while foreign alternative energy companies would be undercut by a lower world oil price.

The system would work even better if we set the price floor at a higher level, such as $90. Demand would fall further, forcing the world oil price down to about $50 a barrel. The variable tariff would then automatically rise to $40, keeping the domestic price up to the $90 target. American refineries would pay $50 for the oil and another $40 for the tariff. Thus, they would pay $90 a barrel but foreign oil companies such as those in Saudi Arabia, Iran, Venezuela and Russia would get only $50. The higher the domestic price floor, the larger the tax rebate going to American families. The variable tariff stabilizes oil prices by dampening both upward and downward price changes.

Will this violate World Trade Organization rules? Possibly. If so, this would give the petro-dictators the right to retaliate by imposing tariffs on their imports. Since these oil-exporting countries produce little else, such tariffs would generate internal inflation, not jobs. Consequently, they are unlikely to impose import restrictions. Their imports are an insignificant portion of our total exports in any case. Their more likely response would be another OPEC attempt at production cuts.

Let's give alternative energy a chance to succeed. If we drop the 54-cent-a-gallon tariff on imported ethanol and pass a flex-fuel mandate, prices at the pump would drop quickly as more ethanol is used. A $40 coupon towards a flex-fuel conversion kit for used cars would also help. New ways of producing ethanol from waste products will help, too.

This is not your typical case of static analysis from your Econ101 course. We are at a tipping-point between old energy solutions and new ones. China has grasped the significance of this moment and is pushing ahead rapidly on developing new energy solutions. If we don't act now we will be left behind to buy new energy products from China along with everything else.

The best way to generate more jobs is to expand old businesses and create new ones. A sudden increase in business energy investments under the umbrella of a guaranteed 10-year foreign crude oil price floor of $80 will be a big help. It will more than offset the mild effects of a slightly higher price at the pump than might otherwise be the case when world crude oil prices fall suddenly. Having a job is more important than having to pay some minimum price at the pump (the price floor) as world oil prices drop. Now is the time to expand our existing energy investments and create many new ones.

You also have to take into account the lives of our soldiers and all the money that we spend overseas to protect foreign sources of oil. An oil tariff price wedge will reduce our demand for foreign oil and reduce (eventually eliminate) our need to protect foreign oil sources. Less military expenditures mean a smaller budget deficit and lower long-term debt. Many countries such as France, Germany, Denmark, Brazil, China and Israel are aggressively acting to reduce their dependency on foreign sources of energy. Why leave the USA vulnerable?

When international financial crises or domestic economic slowdowns cause oil prices to fall, we need to keep them up to protect alternative energy. If our lawmakers fail to protect green jobs during occasional market dips, they will condemn America to perpetual foreign oil addiction. Why wait and watch more alternative energy companies go bankrupt? Congress won't act until you contact your representatives and tell them you favor placing a price floor on crude oil imports to help us break out of this foreign oil addiction trap.[6]

Carbon tax better than trying to pick alternative-energy winner

Should we let Congress pick the next big thing in alternative energy? Will its pet projects save the day, or turn out to be losers that crash and burn?

Perhaps there's a better way. The fundamental problem is our failure to account for unwanted side effects, which economists call *negative externalities,* such as pollution and our dependence on fossil fuels and foreign oil imports. We all pay a price for these negative externalities through the inefficient allocation of our resources.

For a product to be produced efficiently, the full costs and benefits of producing it must exactly match the private costs and benefits the firm uses to calculate its profits. If not all costs and benefits are taken into account, the firm will over produce and generate negative externalities or under produce and generate positive externalities. An example of a *positive externality* would be the protection your friends and colleagues get when you get vaccinated for a readily-transmitted disease, which is why most societies subsidize vaccinations to some extent.

Without the right size tax or subsidy, negative externalities set price below the economically efficient price while positive externalities set price above the optimal price, resulting in what economists call *market failure.*

(1.) ENERGY POLICY

Economists are not against pollution. Pollution is fine as long as it is at its optimal level. The problem is that the current level of pollution is way above its optimal level. Consequently, we need to bring down the pollution level. Environmental and geo-political negative externalities mean that the full cost is often considerably higher than the private cost (the price we now pay). You probably feel that you are already paying too much at the pump. Unfortunately, if the full costs were covered, the pump price would be even higher.

There are two possible approaches to solving this problem. The first approach calls for adding just enough tax to bring the private cost up to the full cost. This first approach would account for the environmental and national security damage caused by buying oil from our adversaries by imposing a tax such as that proposed under the carbon-credit-trading tax system. Alternatively, a second approach brings the full cost down (or the benefits up, depending upon how you look at it) by subsidizing some environmentally friendly form of alternative energy that either we produce or is produced by our geo-political friends.

While this second approach seems less painful, it is also much more dubious. The first approach handicaps carbon polluting forms of energy, and creates a level playing field for alternative energy solutions, making them all considerably more profitable than they are today. The second approach requires that we pick a winner or some subset of possible winners. But how do we choose? What if we are wrong?

Until the late 1700s, the British (and others) suffered severely from not being able to calculate longitude at sea. Ships that used dead-reckoning (straight point-to-point sailing) were attacked by pirates while those deviating from the established sea lanes got lost at sea. The solution that paved the way for the British Empire was not discovered by the usual suspects at Oxford or Cambridge. Instead, a peasant* in the British countryside with almost no formal education solved the problem.[7] He had never even been to sea before devising his solution!

Some think the solution to our energy problem is wind or solar. But wait, maybe there's something better just around the corner. *Bloom Energy* offers a new fuel-pump-like solution based solely on chemical reactions with no burning of fossil fuels. Should we bet our chips on this seemingly cheap solution or is there a fatal flaw or a better method or combination of methods?

Instead, why don't we take the first approach and let the free market sort this all out to find a cost effective solution? Mistakes will be made, but at private expense. Before long, true winners will emerge. Perhaps we should stop screwing around, and just take our carbon tax medicine. Otherwise, we could be sick for quite some time.

An energy plan for Congress: A dynamic self-adjusting price floor for gasoline

Congress faces a difficult dilemma. On one hand, it needs to keep gasoline prices low to avoid burdening already overburdened consumers. On the other hand, it needs to protect green jobs and give alternative energy a chance. Whenever the price of gasoline drops too low, ethanol and other alternative energy companies face bankruptcy. Their products just can't compete with cheap gasoline.

---

* John Harrison,1693-1776, from Barrow-on-Humber in Lincolnshire England.

(1.) ENERGY POLICY

Any future financial crisis anywhere in the world could cause a sudden drop in demand and a fall in gasoline prices such as the drop from over $4 a gallon to around $1.60 a gallon in 2008. The key is to prevent sudden gasoline price dips from forcing alternative energy start-ups into bankruptcy.

Here is a three-point plan for a dynamic, self-adjusting price floor for gasoline that will start out low to avoid hurting consumers while many are still unemployed or underemployed, but will rise along with the demand for gasoline as the economy improves to provide the protection needed to promote green jobs and protect alternative energy:

(1.) *Initially set the price floor at $2.50 per gallon for pure, regular, unleaded gasoline at 87 octane, with corresponding floors for midgrade and premium. Prorate for ethanol mixtures. Since about 46 percent of fuel sold at gas stations in the United States is E10 (gasohol) containing 10 percent ethanol, the actual price at the pump would be a bit less.***

(2.) *At midnight each day, if the average price of pure gasoline is more than $1.25 above the price floor, raise the price floor automatically by 25 cents.*

(3.) *Require that the price floor on pure gasoline never be lowered for the next 10 years.****

** While backed up in traffic or in a parking lot, notice how many cars have the flex-fuel emblem on them. The flex-fuel cars can run on E85 which consists of 85 percent ethanol. Even with a high price for pure gasoline, we could have a low price at the pump for cars running on E85.

*** Alternatively, a soft price floor could be set where gasoline tax rates rise higher and higher as the price of pure gasoline falls below a specified price.

For example, if the average price of pure gasoline has risen just above $4 a gallon, then the price floor for pure gasoline will have risen to $3. See Figure 2 below.

avg. price	$2.50	. . .	$3.75	$3.76	. . .	$4.00	$4.01
price floor	$2.50	. . .	$2.50	$2.75	. . .	$2.75	$3.00

Figure 2. Price floor rises with average gasoline price.

The actual price at the pump could be a lot less if it is mixed with cheaper ethanol. This would happen if Congress got rid of the 54-cent-a-gallon import duty on ethanol.[8] With a price floor of $3 on pure gasoline, you might pay only $2.50 on E10 (10 percent ethanol).

Virtually all cars in Brazil can use E85 which is 85 percent ethanol and a lot cheaper than gasoline when gas prices go sky high. There are currently six million flex-fuel cars in the United States, but there are very few gas stations selling E85. Wal-Mart has been working with Murphy Oil Company to possibly devise a plan to sell E85 at Wal-Mart service stations.[9]

A flex-fuel mandate for new cars would also help us break our dependence on pure gasoline. A used car can be converted to flex-fuel for about $100 in parts including a new computer chip controlling the air mixture, new fittings on the fuel lines and replacing rubber seals with non-rubber seals.

Similar self-adjusting price floors (SAPFs) can be set for diesel, heating oil and similar products.

Consumers will be able to plan ahead knowing that the price of gasoline, heating oil and other petroleum products will not be allowed to fall significantly for the next 10 years from current levels. Potential investors in alternative energy will know that they have 10 years to obtain a good return on their alternative energy investments without having to worry about being undercut by price dips in petroleum products.

This plan will encourage the automobile companies to initially offer more fuel-efficient vehicles and strive to continue improving the fuel efficiency of their products for the next 10 years. Uncertainty is a major factor in inhibiting both short-term expectations and long-term investments in alternative energy. Both families buying fuel efficient cars and companies investing in alternative energy need to know that the era of cheap oil is over.

The United States can take the leadership in reducing greenhouse gas emissions by working with other countries to simultaneously set self-adjusting price floors (SAPFs) for all carbon-emitting products. As an added benefit for the economy as a whole, if deflation begins to pose a serious threat, SAPFs can be used on other key products as well to fend off the deflationary threat which can be very damaging to an economy as seen in Japan.

Law professors propose new gasoline tax with categorical rebates

Law professors Michael Levine and Mark Roe have proposed a tax at the pump with all the tax revenues given back to voters as tax credits or refunds.[10] Each taxpayer would get back the amount of gas tax paid by the average taxpayer. This is similar to my proposal to return crude oil tariffs in as a tax rebate for American families in an earlier section of this chapter.

The new twist offered by Levine and Roe is to allow truckers to get back the average tax paid by truckers and taxis to get back the average tax paid by registered taxis, and so forth for all well-defined fuel-using categories.

Perhaps some categories would be defined by a combination of tonnage and miles driven.

This approach would avoid unduly penalizing occupations such as truck or taxi driving that inherently use more fuel. Rather than treating all drivers equally, dividing drivers into their occupational categories would ensure that we did not discriminate against particular occupations while still discouraging excess fuel consumption within each occupation.

The bad news for people driving gas guzzlers is that they would pay more at the pump in taxes than they would get back. The good news is that fuel-efficient drivers would get back more than they paid. The more you can cut back your gas usage the better this deal becomes. This would further encourage the switch to more fuel efficient technologies.

Throwing more money into the pot from oil tariffs and the sale of carbon credits could sweeten the deal. Under this plan, the average person could get back more than what they paid at the pump. Now that's a deal worth considering.

Financial Times, Tuesday, July 7, 2009 on page 9: "How to make a petrol tax politically viable" by Michael Levine, law professor at New York University School of Law, and Mark Roe, law professor at Harvard Law School.

2. 21ˢᵗ Century Challenges: technology, immigration, newspapers and climate change

P eople who don't like rapid change will not be happy in the 21ˢᵗ century. Like it or not, profound changes are coming. The real questions are: What types of changes can we expect, what will be their impact and how should we prepare for them?

Rising incomes throughout the world have triggered a drop in birth rates in the developed countries. We face rising ranks of retirees and fewer workers contributing to the payroll tax that funds our Social Security and Medicare systems. At the same time people trapped in poverty in less developed countries are seeking work and a path to prosperity. Does immigration offer a win-win solution for both developing and developed countries? Some see a nightmare; others see hope for all.

As countries compete in the technology race, how should they position themselves in that competition? Will the country that wins the most Nobel prizes win the competition? Does the United States have an unexpected comparative advantage as a consequence of our diversity and our unusually venturesome spirit?

Income inequality is often seen as a bad thing. While it may create some problems, it may also offer a way to move ahead more rapidly with new products. Instead of solving our problems by exploiting the rich, perhaps we can just get them to "exploit" themselves. If you can't afford the latest gizmo, don't worry the rich can help you pay for it. This commentary explains how.

Some people believe that modern marketing methods are violating our privacy like never before. Snooping data detectives analyze our every move. Purchases are blocked, or discount coupons extended, by unseen "aliens" who control our lives. It's bad enough when they just record our purchases, but do they really need to infer so much about our family decision making processes and our relationships? Surely, some things should be kept private.

Some journalists are self-selected to shy away from getting too deeply involved with technology. Many majored in college in liberal studies such as English, Art or Music. Most older journalists did not specialize in math, science or engineering. It is especially difficult for the older newspaper people who run the papers to grasp the full implications and possible solutions to the problems posed by the revolution in communication technology. This chapter explores the myths that still haunt many newsrooms and prevent newspapers from making the necessary commitments to survive in the 21st century. We need to understand and appreciate the shift away from one-size-fits-all content delivery and toward the my-size-fits-me demands of their 21st century readers.

Finally, the last commentary addresses the issue of climate change. In particular, it points out that global warming is just one potential climate change problem. There is also the problem of increasingly unpredictable and volatile global weather patterns. Abrupt changes in local weather extremes from hot to cold, wet to dry and calm to extraordinarily windy can make planning for the future difficult and disrupt our lives in ways heretofore totally unexpected. Here again our future is uncertain.

(2.) 21ST CENTURY CHALLENGES

H-1B visas, highly-skilled immigrants and our knowledge economy

Immigration has long played an important role in America. Although immigration has been important in our history, we still need to consider what its impact might be for our economy in the future.

How will openness affect our economy in the long run? The answer depends upon how population changes affect our economy with or without immigration. Statistical studies have revealed the relationship between average income and birth rates. When average incomes rise, birth rates fall. A substantial increase in income per person results in a dramatic drop in birth rates. In fact you might say that the most effective birth control method in the world is per capita income.

Uganda has an annual average income of $1,000 per person. Half of its population is under 15 years old. On the other hand, Japan has an average annual income of $40,000 while 50 percent of Japanese are over 44. In other words, Uganda's median age is 15 while Japan's is 44. Without immigration, the United States and many countries in the European Union would be losing population. Russia's population is already declining. China's one-child policy puts it below the 2.1 replacement rate. The world will eventually face a severe shortage of young people as it becomes more affluent.[1]

The Japanese are trying to deal with this problem without large-scale immigration by introducing ever more sophisticated robots. Just getting a robot to walk turned out to be quite challenging. It seems unlikely that they will be able to replace highly-skilled people with robots any time soon.[2]

41

Nations that find themselves losing population may want to reconsider their opposition to immigration if they want their economies to sustain basic services such as Social Security and Medicare. While immigration can provide more workers and thus more payroll tax revenue, it does much more. Economic studies have shown that immigrants are not random draws from the populations of their home countries. They are self-selected to have imagination, initiative and determination, and progress requires creative people with new ideas. They often play a key role in the establishment of new businesses, new products and in the creation of more jobs.

Rich countries must accept some significant amount of immigration to avoid sliding backward down the economic ladder. As highly skilled jobs become more specialized, companies become choosier. It is no longer enough just to have an advanced degree in statistical analysis. A financial firm may need a specialist in state space models while an internet marketing company may want a Bayesian specialist in decision tree models.[3]

In a free market wages within each specialization are determined by the laws of supply and demand. Whether the real wages of highly skilled workers go up or down depends upon whether the rate of specialization and division of labor is greater than the rate of increase in available workers within each ever-more-narrow specialization. Wages for high-tech workers will go up if the division and specialization of labor is occurring even faster than the rate that such workers are becoming available.

America has a history of attracting hard-working and innovative people. While other nations and groups have continued fighting over land elsewhere in the world, the United States quietly has made off with their best and their brightest. Before 9/11, America led the world in producing both highly educated and highly skilled university graduates. American universities attracted self-selected individuals with exceptional initiative and talent from everywhere. This has enabled America to acquire the most valuable and productive resource of all – highly talented, creative and hardworking people.

As a land of immigrants, America represents people from all sorts of ethnic identities and backgrounds. As a nation, we are not locked into a single, traditional way of doing things. With greater fluidity of labor, openness to new ideas, and better acceptance of people from different cultures and traditions, America has attracted the world's most creative and productive people. This is our true comparative advantage.

Techno-nationalists may hurt, not help America

What if Russia or China earned more Nobel prizes than the United States? Would that be bad? Not necessarily, according to an expert on effective innovation.

Professor Amar Bhidé of Columbia University and author of *The Venturesome Economy* has pointed out in a talk at the Kansas City public library that the ideas that win Nobel prizes usually are easily transferable.[4] A country's economy is more likely to benefit from mid-level or low-level innovations that form the nuts and bolts of technical innovation and are harder to learn.

The risk-taking and creativity of American consumers in their willingness to try new products is another powerful force in favor of the USA. Techno-nationalists pushing for pouring more money into basic research may be sending us in the wrong direction. Such expenditures may be a diversion of funds from mid-level or low-level uses.

Professor Bhidé also pointed out that the total number of local service jobs generated by distributing, selling and maintaining new high-tech products may be much greater than the number of manufacturing or assembly jobs outsourced abroad. At the same time he noted that manufacturing continues to grow in the United States even as manufacturing employment declines. Improvements in productivity explain this paradox.

How the poor exploit the rich

Watching all those fashionable TV shows, but too poor to buy the products advertised? Don't worry; the rich are paying for your entertainment. They are the ones buying those expensive products that keep those TV shows afloat.

In the 21st century many new products require more initial brainpower (fixed costs) and less physical inputs (variable costs) than ever before. As you recall from Econ101, variable costs increase with increasing output, while fixed costs are initial costs that remain unchanged as output increases.

First there was primitive agriculture where variable costs dominated in the form of labor, seed and fertilizer to produce simple, unprocessed products. With no machinery, everything had to be done by hand. More output required more of almost every input.

Then came mechanized agriculture and manufacturing which added some fixed costs to produce processed products. Purchasing costly processing equipment represented a one-time expenditure. Output could vary within a wide range without additional fixed cost equipment expenditures.

Now we move around bits and bytes to produce virtual prototypes (at high fixed cost) whose replication is virtually free (zero variable costs). A smash hit movie may cost millions of dollars to make, but additional copies can be downloaded at little real cost. The fixed costs may be high, but variable cost is virtually zero.

At each stage in our historical economic development, value-added has come to depend more on mental inputs (up-front fixed costs) and less on physical inputs (production-line variable costs). Your free web browser is just the tip of the iceberg. Facebook, MySpace, Twitter, Hi-5 and a host of other networking and gaming sites are free. The rich pay the upfront fixed costs through optional upgrades, services and both online and offline purchases. You can even get Internet access for free. (OK, so you have to sit through a few ads.) Don't you feel sorry for those rich people who have to bear the burden of those initial high fixed costs?

Personal computers used to be very expensive. Back in the day, paying $30,000 for a computer was the norm. Even earlier in grad school, we all chipped in together to get a group discount on calculators that could add, subtract, multiply and divide for a cool $250 a piece. We all hear about the first-mover advantage. What about the first-mover disadvantage? Who's buying those Tesla Motors electric cars at $100,000 a pop?[5] You won't see me in one any time soon. No doubt you feel sorry for those poor rich people who have to cover those fixed costs. Even at a price of $40,000, will the average middle class family be able to afford GM's upcoming "Volt" electric car?[6] No problem; the rich to the rescue. It's just another opportunity to "tax" the rich.

We ruthlessly exploit the rich who don't even realize how much they're being taken. Once the rich have paid all those research and development costs and economies of scale kick in, it's all downhill for the price from there.

Yes, Virginia, there is a Santa Claus (or should we say a Robin Hood) and an upside to income inequality. If you're rich, don't despair; if you act poor, you can exploit the rich, too.

Aliens have taken over Planet Earth

You may think that greedy Wall Street bankers were the cause of our financial crisis, but if you dig deeper, you will discover they were duped by aliens. Aliens (aka "quants") created those highly leveraged financial derivatives that turned our banking system into a house of cards.[7] The aliens are everywhere. They devise complicated schemes to watch your every move and control your life.

At the shopping mall, you use your credit card. As your data are being processed by the computer, an alien is intercepting your information. The alien knows your past purchases including when you shop, where you shop, what you buy and might be expected to buy and in what quantities. In a nanosecond the alien uses an artificial neural network algorithm to calculate the probability that you are you. If you are buying the usual thing, at the usual time and place, no problem. However, if you are trying to purchase something you don't usually buy at an unusual place (for you) at an unusual time (for you), the calculated probability that you are you may fall below the acceptable threshold. The clerk's computer screen flashes "check ID." The aliens have blocked your purchase.[8]

(2.) 21ST CENTURY CHALLENGES

But it doesn't end there. When you finally get that toaster or television home, you find a registration form to fill out and send in. It starts out asking for the model number, date purchased and the price paid. Then it wants to know your mailing address, phone number and email address. Next it needs your age, gender and education. After that it's on to your marital status, income and net worth. At some point you say "enough is enough," and send it in with one or more questions left blank.

Well, at least you thought you left them blank. Don't worry, the aliens have figured out your "type" and will fill in the blanks for you with amazing accuracy.[9] So much for privacy. The aliens know where you live and the value of your home in today's market, even if you don't. Aliens control those special discount coupons printed out on your sales receipts. They know your favorite restaurants and what you like to do in your spare time.

Aliens observe husbands and wives making joint decisions. Couples buy a house; they buy a car; they go out to eat; they have a baby. Aliens can determine whether one or the other partner dominates a particular family decision and how strongly they agree or disagree with one another. Define "fighting" as a negative correlation and "supportive" as a positive correlation. Applying these definitions to joint decisions, aliens can determine if your neighbors are fighting, what they are fighting about, and how intensely they are fighting. I won't even start to tell you about all the stuff the aliens are doing to you over the Internet.

Statistical methods are very powerful and very dangerous. They can be used to clarify or to deceive, for good or for evil. Like Harry Potter, statistical analysts deal with unobservables every day. They are the wizards of the 21st century.

The bottom line is this: If you think you can go through life without being affected by the results of statistical methods and statistical analysis, forget it. You are on the wrong planet. The aliens have already taken over this one.

Four myths about newspapers and online advertising

Four myths persist concerning traditional and online newspapers and online advertising generally:

Myth #1: *Young people will become interested in reading traditional newspapers when they get older.*

There are several variations of this myth but they all boil down to a pipe-dream by "the greatest generation" that young people will eventually become just like them. For better or worse, what worked in the 20th century will not necessarily work in the 21st.

This first myth is a misconception based on the ideas of Vance Packard in his books *The Hidden Persuaders*(1957)[10] and *The Status Seekers*(1959)[11]. Along with John Kenneth Galbraith[12], Packard promoted the idea that big business just created products and then used Madison Avenue advertising companies to brainwash consumers into buying those products. This no longer works. The old ABC-NBC-CBS oligopoly on television advertising has broken down. No torrent of broadcast and print advertising will convince young people to read traditional newspapers.

(2.) 21ST CENTURY CHALLENGES

> **Myth #2:** *Media brand and quality will win out over free content.*

For the typical newspaper targeting the general reader, this is a myth. This only works for limited, niche markets with relatively wealthy readers. Perhaps, *The New York Times, The Wall Street Journal, The Financial Times, Investors' Business Daily* and a few other papers can pull this off to some degree, but generally speaking most newspapers will not be able to survive by charging for content.

Traditionally newspapers had monopolies in smaller cities and oligopolies in larger ones. Now with online news, the marginal cost of replication and delivery is essentially zero so the old monopoly-oligopoly model is dead. Pictures and news about that local soccer game, high school reunion or graduation are readily available from any number of your hundreds of local *Facebook* friends. Online blogs are providing innumerable news analyses, some of rather high quality. Economics will drive price down to zero to match the marginal cost of newspaper content. Competition for advertising dollars is getting more intense as advertisers discover more effective placement of their ads elsewhere. *Craigslist* has "stolen away" local classified ads, further undercutting one of the principal sources of newspaper revenue.

> **Myth #3:** *Traditional demographic advertisement targeting will work online.*

Most off-line advertising is based on demographics. Fair Isaac and other companies serving the advertising industry have devised elaborate socio-economic strata to pigeon-hole consumers into appropriate target categories defined by demographic group and geographic area.[13] These traditional advertising methods worked in an era of economic, social and racial segregation. Society today is becoming too diverse and too integrated to target people by race, income or ethnicity. Moreover, choices have become more diverse as products become more individualized with customized content. At a bare minimum advertising online requires behavioral targeting that uses IP-addresses and browser *cookies*.

Myth #4: *Privacy concerns will prevent effective ad targeting.*

As a rule, old people are driven by fear while young people are driven by hope. Older folks are worried about losing their life savings to identity thieves and online scam artists.* Young people just want to interact with their friends.

For young people the problem with online advertising is not that it violates their privacy or even that it violates their space. Their concern is that online advertising is more often than not, irrelevant. It is not that they object to online advertising in principle. What they object to is the poor online advertising targeting. If advertisers would just send them the specific ads they want to see and drop the rest, most young folks would have no beef with online ads.

---

* Normally analysts creating collaborative filters have no use for and usually delete any information that would uniquely identify an individual by name.

(2.) 21ST CENTURY CHALLENGES

Revealed preference "Daily Me" key to online newspaper survival

The individualized newspaper that autonomously detects each reader's personal preferences is coming soon. The new online newspaper approach of allowing each reader to customize the display by selecting topics or phrases that interest them is a first step but is not sufficient for a newspaper's long-term survival.

Until the 1940s economists thought that the only way to determine a person's precise preference map was to ask them their preferences. This proved to produce a very imprecise and inaccurate preference map. When his Harvard economics professor explained that this was unfortunately the only viable approach, graduate student Paul Samuelson claimed to have a better way.[14] He called his new method *revealed preference*. Samuelson went on to become an MIT professor and Nobel Prize laureate in economics.

Proving your professor wrong has become a time honored tradition, but proving traditional newspapers wrong may take a bit more explaining. The key to the success of revealed preference is that it focuses on what a person actually does and not on what they say they want or expect to do. Behavioral targeting is essential to giving readers what they really want. As an economist I don't care what you say, I just want to see what you actually purchase with your money. With online news, time is money. You reveal your news preferences when you reveal what you spend your time reading.

It's not that traditional newspapers are actually taking the wrong approach; it is just inadequate. A much better approach is Amazon's collaborative filter method.[15] Following Amazon's approach to book recommendations,

51

newspapers could suggest news and commentary by first observing what a particular reader rates highly. Then suggest other news and commentary based on what other readers with similar tastes have enjoyed.

Netflix has used this approach to offering its customers movie recommendations. In the fall of 2006 Netflix CEO Reed Hastings offered $1 million dollars to anyone who could improve Netflix's recommendation system by 10 percent. On Sept. 21, 2009, a group of seven scientists and engineers won the prize in a competition with 51,000 contestants from 186 countries.[16]

At least one example exists of using the revealed preference/collaborative filter approach to suggesting news stories for readers. Eduardo Hauser, CEO of DailyMe.com reports that his online aggregator "has been developing news personalization and recommendation technology since 2006." Google News allows readers to select news topics of interest and has demonstrated its ability to use collaborative filters or other such statistical methods to present readers with suggested news stories based on their individual preferences.

In the long run online newspapers will not be profitable if they don't understand the difference between what readers say they want and what they really want. Asking a reader's preferences may be a good first step, but it is not sufficient.

A newspaper that is serious about surviving online must go further and observe where the readers really spend their time, and ultimately, their online money. Newspapers that ignore the need for online behavioral targeting will themselves ultimately be ignored.

Traditionally newspapers attracted people with exceptional writing skills but not technical skills. Older leaders in the news business do not always fully

understand sophisticated behavioral targeting strategies
and how to monetize them.

There is a dark side to all this. Traditional
newspapers expose a reader to a wide variety of news and
commentary. Readers who focus on their own narrow
interests may become uninformed voters and poor
citizens. If readers concentrate their interests and only
see and read what they really want, they may become like
the professor becoming increasingly specialized in his or
her field who learns more and more about less and less
until they know everything about nothing.

Is there more to our climate problems than just global warming?

Perhaps our climate problems are bigger than just global
warming. Is our climate losing its inherent stability and
beginning to cycle between extremes? Are we altering the
variability of our climate and not just its average
temperature?

For several years the Southeast suffered drought
conditions with Georgia, Alabama and Florida fighting
over access to water. Lately they are getting hit with more
water than they can handle -- lots of flooding. Coming
back from Alabama over the holiday we found water
coming close to flooding out some of the interstate
highways in the South.

Is human activity on our planet making our climate
less stable? Global climate variation may turn out to be a
more important issue than the global warming one. At
least with global warming we can anticipate the effects of
gradual warming and prepare for them. But how do we
prepare for dramatic variations from hot to cold, dry to

wet and a sudden increase in tornadoes, hurricanes, cyclones and tsunamis?[17]

A stable climate is like a sine or cosine curve with a big wavelength and a small amplitude. Such a curve rises slowly to a modest height. On the other hand, an unstable climate looks like a curve swinging frequently between extremes. If our climate amplitude is increasing and our climate wavelength is shortening, we may be in for a rough ride. When it comes to our climate problems, global warming may be just the tip of the iceberg.

3. Education: confronting old issues and new developments

E ducation is facing dramatic changes in response to the challenges and opportunities provided by the 21st century. Big changes are coming whether we are ready or not. We can rise to the occasion by stepping back and gaining a broad understanding of the new reality and then devising new, more effective strategies, or we can continue pursuing old methods that take a more narrow approach to our educational issues.

This chapter offers a broader perspective to understanding the changes that are taking place in the process by which young people learn about the world. It argues for a more imaginative approach to education including the use of the latest technologies that are being so enthusiastically embraced by our children and grandchildren. Students are highly motivated in their desire to be winners but find video games a more rewarding experience that schoolwork. Understanding student motivation and providing the right incentives are the keys to success in transforming our educational system.

With all these changes there is still room for tradition. Notre Dame has been willing to honor people who have made significant contributions even when some of their beliefs are contrary to those of the Catholic Church. President Obama has emphasized the need to find common ground by looking for points of agreement, instead of focusing on our differences. Learning requires openness to new ideas and new ways of thinking, while retaining valuable traditions.

Flynn Effect, IQ scores and SAT scores: Are our children smarter than we are?

If the SAT scores of our children are lower than ours were, how can we explain IQ scores rising at 3 points per decade? This *Flynn Effect* is well-known but not easily explained.[1] Your kids may think they're smarter than you are. Are they right?

James R. Flynn, professor emeritus at the University of Otago in New Zealand and the author who hypothesized the *Flynn Effect*, has argued that people's environmental circumstances have a substantial effect on their IQ scores.[2] Throughout history people have allocated their mental energy according to their priorities, as determined by their attitudes, which, in turn, reflect their circumstances. Both SAT scores and IQ scores ultimately may reflect our historical circumstances.

Consider the lower SAT scores. When I was in college in 1967 the average overall SAT score was 1,059. By 2008 the average had dropped to 1,017. When I was a kid, there were no hand calculators. In grad school I was glad to pay $250 for a calculator that was pretty much limited to addition, subtraction, multiplication and division. Why should kids today work hard to learn basic math when the answers are readily available at the click of a button? With today's information overload, why learn history when Wikipedia can easily provide even the most arcane historical facts?

Born during the Roosevelt administration, I didn't have the advantage of inter-library loan, much less the Internet, so I learned to hold on to every book and bit of information I could get. Today, why memorize some fact when you can always just "Google it?"

(3.) EDUCATION

After retiring from 30 years of teaching, I took a job for just over a year at *Adknowledge, Inc.*, an Internet advertising firm in Kansas City where many people, including CEO Scott Lynn,[3] were in their 20s. My desk was full of papers in contrast to the clean and clear desks of my younger colleagues. In my day, information was hard to come by. I was trained to hold on to every useful piece of information. Today, memorizing facts and holding on to papers is not necessary, since most facts can be retrieved at the click of a mouse.

Older folks like me may have scored well on the SAT not because we were smart, but because our attitudes and priorities caused us to retain lots of facts useful on the SAT but not so relevant for the IQ test.

What about the rising IQ scores? IQ scores are re-centered at 100 points every so often to reflect the average intelligence of the current generation, but Professor Flynn re-adjusted IQ scores to make them comparable across generations. Using the adjusted data, Flynn discovered that IQ scores have been rising at 3 points a decade. This implies that people on average now do better at answering essentially the same questions than people from earlier generations did.

In August 2008 on xanga.com commentator "pnrj" projected IQ scores back in time along a linear path.[4] The backward linear projection of the *Flynn Effect* implies that the average person in Albert Einstein's generation (born 1879) would have an IQ of 74 or "severely mentally retarded" in today's parlance. William Shakespeare's contemporaries (born 1564) with an average IQ of 28 would be about as intelligent as a smart dog, and so forth. Of course, this makes no sense. Unlike Flynn's flat rate, the true rate must be increasing over time on a curved path as shown in Figure 3 at the end of this section.

How can circumstances that shape our attitudes and priorities explain this *Flynn Effect*? Our brains currently use about 25 percent of the calories we consume. During earlier times, when humans were under greater stress, it would have been foolish to waste a great deal of time and mental energy engaged in abstract thinking. At blogs.psychologytoday.com Scott Barry Kaufman (www.scottbarrykaufman.com), who specializes in studying intelligence and creativity, provides this clue[5] in recounting psychologist Alexander Luria's interview in the early 20th century with a peasant in a remote region of the Soviet Union:[6]

IQ Test Examiner: All bears are white where there is always snow; in Novaya Zemiya there is always snow; what color are the bears there?

Soviet Union Peasant: I have seen only black bears and I do not talk of what I have not seen.

IQ Test Examiner: But what do my words imply?

Soviet Union Peasant: If a person has not been there he cannot say anything on the basis of words. If a man was 60 or 80 and had seen a white bear there and told me about it, he could be believed.

From the point of view of the Soviet peasant, it was a waste of time to allocate mental energy to thinking about an abstraction far from the reality of that peasant's circumstances. Historically most people never traveled far from where they were born. In earlier times, people as individuals and society as a whole could not afford to engage in abstract thinking. They needed to focus on survival, which could not be taken for granted.

Until the second half of the 18th century most people were extremely poor. Their occupations and tribal villages were generally limited to those of their parents. Developing their minds by thinking about abstract concepts was just not in the cards. Aristotle and Galileo were exceptions. They had powerful patrons who sponsored them to give them time for abstract thinking.

For most people knowing their place in society and not challenging their assigned place in society was the safest path to follow. Even today there are those who resent someone who seems "too big for their britches" in talking too much about abstract concepts.

Although we cannot measure the IQ scores of our ancestors, it is quite likely that average IQ scores rose only very gradually until the late 18th century until the industrial revolution began to liberate more and more people from the drudgery of the daily fight for survival.

Only with increasing real incomes were people able to increase their IQ's substantially. In other words, it has not been a linear progression. The rate of increase in IQs may not have been at the constant 3 points a decade rate claimed by the *Flynn Effect*, but may be increasing at an increasing rate. This means that the IQs back in the days of Shakespeare and Einstein may have been higher than the backwards linear projections provided by "pnrj" imply. It also means that future increases in IQ scores could well exceed the 3 points per decade rate as our grandsons and granddaughters get more involved in abstract thinking.

Figure 3 below compares the *Flynn Effect* represented by the straight line with the true effect represented by the curved line which starts out essentially flat and then curves dramatically upward.

The repetitive jobs of the past are being off-shored and off-loaded to automated, voice-activated semi-intelligent systems. In the future physically demanding work will be done by robots. Our children and grandchildren will need to think more intelligently and more creatively just to keep a decent job.

Are your children and grandchildren smarter than you are? They had better be, or they are doomed.

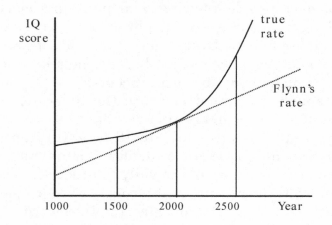

Figure 3. Flynn's rate versus true rate

Google Books changes everything in student teacher education

A nation has an infinite number of possible histories. There is only one history that happened, and many histories that didn't happen. If America is to lead the world throughout the 21st century and beyond, we must grasp the full implication of the Internet now and fundamentally change our education system.

(3.) EDUCATION

Towards the end of the 19th century and the beginning of the 20th century there were two nations in the western hemisphere that were poised to be great world leaders. They had roughly the same wealth in national resources and GDP per person, and the same number of people with about the same level of education.

One of them made it, and the other one didn't. What happened to our competitor and why were we so successful? Were we just lucky?

In the late 1800s and early 1900s two countries looked to great broad plains extending far to the west until reaching high distant mountains. It was a vast unexplored territory just as the Internet now seems to our students and teachers. These two countries were among the top ten richest countries in the world with millions of immigrants pouring in. Would Argentina leave the United States far in the dust or vice versa? [7]

The key to our success can be summed up in one word: *empowerment.* Both Argentina and the United States had powerful elites that controlled their economies. As their most energetic and adventurous people moved westward, the United States *empowered* its people by giving out small parcels of land while Argentina gave its land to its elite.

We now face a critical point in human history. Access to the Internet is spreading rapidly throughout the world. Even poor people who never had access to anything beyond their isolated village have suddenly gained access to the Internet.

The country that grasps the full implications of the Internet for the *empowerment* of its citizens will lead in the 21st century and beyond. The United States must rise to meet this challenge. We can no longer afford the Little-House-on-the-Prairie approach to education where students just recite what the teacher says instead of learning how to figure things out on their own.

Google Books changes everything. Teachers are no longer the ultimate source of knowledge. The Internet is. We no longer have to restrict ourselves to a single textbook. Google Books is our textbook.

It is not enough to learn facts. Students must also learn how to formulate their own strategies. Don't teach health; teach how to create your own personal health strategy. Instead of teaching how to acquire wealth, teach how to develop your own individual wealth strategy. This gives students ownership of their strategies and the ability to change their strategies as circumstances change. Now more than ever, our students need motivation and inspiration, and, above all, *empowerment.*

It all starts in Baby College. Baby College operates in Harlem and elsewhere. Social science research has revealed the enormous power of *empowerment.* Baby College teaches parents how to empower their children to feel free to explore and experiment.[8] It's one thing if your child is about to catch fire or fall off a cliff, but is it really necessary to keep saying: "don't touch this" or "don't do that"? The natural inclination of children to explore and experiment is too often suppressed.

Everything is exciting and sometimes scary to a baby because it is new and unknown. Once all the basics are learned, they want to continue with the excitement of learning so they seek fantasy worlds where there are still new and unexpected things to learn. This means that young people get bored without the stimulation of new, mysterious and exciting new things to learn. Teachers must encourage exploration and experimentation on the Internet. *Empower* children to get to know other people in other cultures with new and different ideas. Don't let your child's natural desire to learn die from disuse, discouragement or lack of stimulation.

Too often we get intellectually lazy as we mature and lock into left-wing and right-wing platitudes instead of expending the mental energy to examine each new proposal on its merits. After reading a book presenting a right-wing point of view, it is good to then read a left-wing book on the same subject, to keep your mind sharp so you can continue to field balls coming at you from different directions. *Empowering* our children to think for themselves and to continue to explore the ever changing world of ideas can help them avoid mental atrophy. It's not just China; we could find ourselves left behind by Brazil and many other countries if we don't wake up soon and change our approach to education.

Spend some of those millions for educational video games

The U.S. Department of Education scheduled $650 million for 2010 and an additional $500 million in 2011 to provide incentives for innovations in education.[9] The money goes to innovative school districts and nonprofit organizations that come up with new ideas to enhance our educational system. Now is the time to think in bigger, bolder terms.

Economics is all about motivation and incentives. Marxism failed because it didn't recognize the importance of incentives. Business is all about motivating the customer to buy a product or service. What is needed in education is insight into what motivates today's students and how to direct all that energy toward education.

In teaching introductory statistics to students at the University of Notre Dame, I used a homework system called *"Adventures in Statistics."*[10] This electronic interactive homework system challenged students and tapped into their desire to be a winner while demonstrating their mastery of a topic. There is a module for each topic covered in the course.

In the *Adventures* "game," students can select a tutorial to learn how to play or try example games. Students are confronted with questions and data to work out the answers with pencil, paper and a hand calculator. Two students working next to one another on adjacent computers face slightly different questions and the random number generator gives them different samples.

After practicing, the student advances to certification mode. If a student fails to answer correctly with at least two decimal places of accuracy, a new sample is drawn for the student to try again. Students must answer all questions correctly before they can get certified for that homework.

Adventures provides instant feedback and does not permit incomplete or sloppy homework. Students have to keep trying with reworded questions and new samples until they get it right. Everyone's ultimately a winner. It's just that some are winners a lot sooner than others.

Before each class the teacher can monitor how much time each student is taking in solving each problem. Teachers can then adjust their lectures to address areas of general weakness, but also identify an individual student who is having difficulty with a particular concept to help after class.[11]

From "Dancing with the Stars" to "American Idol" and all those game shows, it's all about being a winner. American children today are being bombarded with the message: "You've got to be a winner." No surprise that our kids spend endless hours playing video games. Lots of people are already addicted to Sudoku just as some are to crossword puzzles.

We need to promote *"Adventures in Statistics," "Adventures in Mathematics," "Adventures in English Literature," "Adventures in Learning Spanish,"* et cetera.

The million dollar prize for the competition to enhance Netflix's movie recommendation system drew entries from 51,000 contestants from 186 countries. Surely a contest to create educational video games would also draw a large number of contestants, especially if the winners were allowed to earn royalties, which was not the case in the Netflix competition.[12]

Some adults don't like this idea. After all the pain and effort they went through to pass math class, it doesn't seem fair that their children might actually have fun learning math. It's like those cereals that are good for you. They're not supposed to taste good. Somehow tasting good while being nutritious is cheating.

It is unfortunate that just being virtuous is not a sufficiently strong motivating force. If it were, then the mantra "from those according to their abilities to those according to their needs" may have worked.

Instead we must face the reality of what drives student motivation and energy. Yes, we need to invest heavily into exciting video games that both "taste good" and provide lots of educational "nutrition" as well.

Once schools start purchasing such educational video game homework systems, software companies will bombard them with competing offerings just as they do with textbooks. With the right monetary incentives our private, free enterprise system will kick into full gear. Then we will begin to see some very inventive and very exciting educational video games.

In our educational system, as in our economic system, if we get the incentives right, we will get the outcomes we want.

New math can succeed
with right attitude and priorities

Many attempts have been made in the past to introduce the "new math" into our schools. In theory the "new math" conceptual approach is much better than the traditional "memorize and drill" approach to learning mathematics. Educational strategies that focus on a mechanical approach to learning facilitate teaching to the test and cheating by teachers under pressure to meet student test score targets.[13] A key problem is ensuring that the teacher really understands the conceptual approach and has the necessary teaching skills and demeanor to transfer those concepts to the students. This aspect is critical and often insurmountable.

Math is very interesting. If you square a number greater than one, it gets bigger. But if you square a number between zero and one, it gets smaller. That is strange and unexpected, but it turns out to be a critical fact in the stability of dynamic systems. It's somewhat analogous to the fact that many substances contract as they get colder, but when water turns to ice it expands. The Egyptians made good use of this fact when they split off the blocks of stone to build the pyramids.

Two important keys to success in education are attitude and priority. You start with attitude. Both teacher and student must be convinced that math is interesting and fun (and ultimately useful, as well). Do teacher and student believe in what they are doing or are they just following orders? If students understand the conceptual purpose of the math, they can solve problems that the memorizers will never be able to solve.

Priority may be even more important. What is important in life and what is not? If you don't believe in the importance of math in enabling you to succeed in life, you are not likely to master the new math (or even the old math). Math requires commitment, focus and a great deal of mental energy. When doing math, pretend that you are doing surgery on your best friend, or crossing a field full of land mines. Be very careful.

What many people do not realize is that they are fully capable of programming themselves for success or failure. The subconscious mind is nothing more than the accumulation of thoughts that we have drilled into our minds on a day-to-day basis. When I was a clerk at a battalion headquarters at Fort Knox, a new second lieutenant joined the office. He had just gotten married. Every day he had something bad to say about his new wife. It could be as minor as: "She burned the toast." After a year he got divorced. No surprise. Students taking a required stats class can either say to themselves "Mathematics is boring" or they can say "At times math can seem strange and mysterious, but it is fun and really interesting." Bombarding yourself with internal and external messages about the importance and positive aspects of mathematics is the key to success.

If mother, father, teacher and child all have the right attitude and priorities, then the "new math" conceptual approach can be far superior. They've got to believe in what they're doing and really want to do it.
If not, it can be a complete disaster.

Espresso Book Machine offers hot book with your coffee

*On Demand Books** has partnered with *Google Books* to sell an *Espresso Book Machine*[14] that can print and bind a 300-page paperback book with full-color cover in 4 minutes for a suggested retail price of $8 per book. You can now purchase books literally hot off the press.[15]

Google has worked with libraries to identify and digitize over 2 million out-of-copyright books. *On Demand Books* has an additional 1.6 million books to bring the total books available for printing on the *Espresso Book Machine* to 3.6 million. They range from old popular classics to obscure, largely unknown books from the past. Some may have wide appeal while others may appeal only to people with rather narrow, specialized interests.**

Bookstores are taking the bait and starting to order these $100,000 machines. Along with the advent of ebooks, this may bring about their own destruction.

Harvard Book Store owner Jeffrey Mayersohn installed an *Espresso Book Machine* to provide his customers with a wide range of classic books. Ironically his private bookstore is located along Massachusetts Avenue close to the Harvard University's *Widener Library* by Harvard Yard in Cambridge, MA. The old, out-of-date books were the last vestige of traditional libraries in the Internet age where "visiting the library," more often than not, just means going to the library's website.

The first *Espresso Book Machine* to appear on the West Coast of the United States was installed in *Village Books* in Fairhaven just south of Bellingham,

---

* www.ondemandbooks.com
** www.ondemandbooks.com/EBM_Brochure.pdf

Washington. Clearly this is just the beginning of a revolution in print-on-demand book publication.

Why stop at bookstores? *Starbucks* will want to offer you a book to read with your latte. Airports along with bus and train stations may be next. Could *McDonalds* be far behind?

The first prototype of a machine to print, bind and trim on-demand books was developed 10 years ago by Jeff Marsh (nice name, but not related) of Lebanon, Missouri. The World Bank's Info Shop in Washington, D.C. was the first to try out his machine in April of 2006.***

Initially a few wealthy people will order *Espresso Book Machines* for their homes. Inevitably the price of the machines will fall and demand will spread. The cost of the paper, ink and binding materials is already as low as $3 for a 300-page book. Soon manufactures of computer printers will want in on the action and add binding to their printer's set of tricks. Bookstores may be sorry they got this ball rolling.

Obama honorary degree consistent with Notre Dame traditions

The University of Notre Dame recently awarded an honorary degree to President Obama in spite of his support of abortion rights. Notre Dame has a long tradition of awarding honorary degrees to people with a wide range of religious beliefs and political positions. Was it wrong for Notre Dame to award an abortion rights supporter an honorary degree?

Non-Catholics have always played important roles at Notre Dame. As early as the late 1970s a team of five

---

*** http://web.worldbank.org => InfoShop => Espresso Printing non-Catholic Notre Dame faculty members worked to assist the Catholic Diocese of Cleveland with their high school enrollment and financial problems. Notre Dame's previous provost, Nathan Hatch, was a non-Catholic and served Notre Dame for many years with great distinction.

Awarding honorary degrees to non-Catholics who hold beliefs at odds with most Catholics is nothing new. President Obama is certainly not the first to be so honored.

In 2002 as a Notre Dame faculty member, I served on Notre Dame's College of Arts and Letters Honorary Degree Committee with two other faculty members to recommend honorary degree recipients for the 2003 commencement. Along with my two colleagues on the committee I was glad to recommend a Jewish scholar for an honorary degree. The college and university agreed.

Our recommendation was well within Notre Dame's tradition of occasionally awarding an honorary degree to someone whose beliefs were contrary not only to most Catholics, but in some cases, contrary to all Catholics. How can it be okay to award an honorary degree to a person who does not recognize the divinity of Christ, but not okay to award one to someone who might have a different conception about conception? Why should Christ's divinity have to take a back seat to the disagreement over when a fetus becomes a child?

Notre Dame should continue its tradition of awarding honorary degrees to people who have made important contributions even if they happen to hold some beliefs entirely contrary to those of the Catholic Church.[16]

4. Economic Theory:
new challenges to old paradigm

This chapter focuses on the evolution of economic theory and practice as well as on some renowned economists who have brought about significant changes to the dismal science. Economists face new challenges as the very nature of our economy changes. The large manufacturing labor markets and routine professional jobs are giving way to more creative, small-enterprise work environments.

Automation and off-shoring are just part of the picture. While big businesses consolidate, their existence is being undermined by new, small-scale production and communication capabilities. Small businesses are springing up that make use of the Internet for assistance in production, marketing and distribution of their products and services. New products and services are being introduced more quickly than ever before. We are, as author Daniel Pink says, becoming a "Free Agent Nation."

Behavioral economists provide more and more examples of apparent irrationality in economics in contradiction to the rationality assumption of traditional economics. What they have failed to fully comprehend is the role of mental energy in explaining human behavior. As brain scanning becomes more widespread, we can expect economists to finally grasp the mental constraints that prevent everyone everywhere from "doing the math" consistent with rational choice theory. As medical technicians record brain inputs and outputs, we can finally start to make precise measurements of mental activity to allow us to create markets for mental energy.

71

Job losses may be permanent

As our economy pulled out of the 2008-2009 recession, many companies were not too keen on rehiring the large numbers of employees that they laid off. Manufacturers have retooled for more extensive automation and have continued outsourcing wherever possible. Firms formerly employing large numbers of professional workers have made greater use of technology to improve the productivity of their remaining workers, and filled in with temporary workers wherever necessary.

In the early days of our republic, our unemployment rate appears to have been generally lower than that of most European countries. Even up until the beginning of the industrial revolution in Britain and beyond, we generally relied on self-employment for our jobs. Farming was the primary occupation. When local conditions and markets soured, our rugged individualists just moved on to the western frontier.

Nowadays the frontier is the Internet with its World Wide Web. Just as the industrial revolution changed work from self-employment to a company job, the Internet is reversing the process as more and more individuals sell on e-Bay and Amazon in response to long-term job loss or for added income. With long-term unemployment on the rise, more and more unemployed are finding their own way to make a buck.

There was a time when movies in Hollywood were created by only a few big entertainment companies. Today quite a few famous actors have chosen to become producers by attracting investor capital and appropriate talent to make their own multimillion dollar movies. These individual projects are typical of our new do-it-yourself, entrepreneurial generation.

(4.) ECONOMIC THEORY

The future that Marx and Engels saw when they produced their *Communist Manifesto* in 1848 is no longer the future we face as more people gain control of their own work hours and conditions.[1] Government has increasingly taken over the responsibility for health, safety and retirement from unions, which have declined as service jobs, small business employment and self-employment have risen.

At the same time companies are not what they used to be. The highly vertically integrated company is being replaced with one that relies more and more on outsourcing and just-in-time delivery to meet the specific needs of specific customers. Dell Computer's Design Studio provides the "classic" example of customization in designing your own laptop followed by outsourcing to produce and deliver it.

For better or for worse this recent recession is serving as a catalyst to move us toward what Daniel Pink refers to as the *Free Agent Nation* in his book by the same name.[2] Ultimately many of us will be forced to face the same reality cavemen and cavewomen all faced, namely, if you want a job you may just have to create your own.

Restoring the efficiency of free markets

Economics is the science of figuring out how scarce resources should be used to maximize our well-being. This means determining production, distribution and consumption. Free markets have been seen as the answer to this problem ever since the fall of the Soviet Union in what Francis Fukuyama called "the end of history" in his book *The End of History and the Last Man*.[3]

73

What many people do not realize is that economists have long recognized the failure of free markets to produce optimal results in a number of different circumstances. In theory, relative price differences should accurately reflect relative differences in costs in production and benefits in consumption between two products. If a price fails to reflect the product's true costs and benefits, that price distortion causes a misallocation of resources.

For example, when one company gains a monopoly in the production or distribution of a product or service, economists recognize that as a market failure. In a competitive market, production increases to the point where competition forces the price down to just cover the cost of producing and selling the last unit. In the absence of competitors, a monopolist can maximize its profits by withholding output and forcing up the price of its product. The monopolist takes some of the benefit that would have gone to consumers and keeps it for itself. Economists recognize that the price for that product has been set too high. Their solution is to bring in competitors (free trade) to force that price back down.[4]

In other circumstances, economists declare market failure because a price has been set too low. For example, a *negative externality* occurs when the cost of producing and consuming a product does not incorporate the resources lost due to water pollution or air pollution. The price of the product is set too low if the costs used in a company's profit calculations do not include the cost to society of that environmental damage. Economists usually recommend taxing the product by an amount that corresponds to the value of the resources foregone to correct this form of market failure and bring the price up to its appropriate level.

The free-market system is not particularly designed to benefit companies or their workers. When a new profitable opportunity arises, a company with first-mover advantage can take advantage of the opportunity to make economic profits (i.e., above average business profits). However, in the long run with unrestricted entry and new substitute products, companies compete among themselves to drive prices down to just barely cover the cost of the last unit sold. Workers compete among themselves to drive wages down to just barely cover their investments in their education and jobs skills. At the end of the day, consumers, who have done nothing except sit and watch from the sidelines, get most of the benefit from free markets. The consumer is king! or queen! That is good news and the most democratic outcome we could hope for because we are all consumers.

Paul Samuelson played a key role in the development of modern economics

Before Paul Samuelson, economics was largely anecdotes and stories supplemented with some simple charts and graphs. Samuelson brought rigor and discipline to the subject. His 1941 Harvard Ph.D. dissertation, first published in 1947, created a mathematical approach to economics that by the mid-1960s had transformed the entire economics profession.

It would be hard to overstate Paul Samuelson's role in economics. Both his critics and supporters recognize his profound impact. His supporters argue that by making economics more mathematical, he forced economists to define their jargon more precisely and to put their contentions in the form of testable hypotheses. In doing so he made economics conform to the rules of scientific investigation where theory is rigorously tested with empirical evidence.

Samuelson's critics argue that he began a process whereby economists borrowed mathematical tools from physics that were not appropriate for economics and were left behind when other scientific disciplines moved on to incorporate more complex, dynamical systems into their disciplines. For example see Philip Mirowski's book *More Heat than Light*.[5] Other critics say that Samuelson's approach left little room for the important role of institutions in economics.

For example, Samuelson's approach allowed for the development of modern labor economics which focuses on workers employing their human capital and selling their labor services on the basis of their labor productivity. In contrast, traditional institutional economics focuses on the struggle between labor and business for profits with unions and government regulations playing a key role in that struggle.

In consumer behavior theory Samuelson contributed the key concept of *revealed preference*.[6] Unlike psychologists, who might be more interested in asking people why they behave the way they do, economists tend to focus on the bottom line. Before Samuelson, economists assumed, like psychologists, that the only way to discover people's preferences was to ask them. Samuelson showed that people's preference functions can be derived by observing their behavior and employing mathematical rules like transitivity, which says if people prefer A to B and B to C then they must also prefer A to C. Asking them their preferences often produced misleading and incomplete information, but observing their behavior produced more reliable predictions.

Samuelson alienated conservatives by endorsing policies proposed by John Maynard Keynes[7] and opposed by Milton Friedman[8] to manipulate monetary and fiscal policies in an attempt to control the economy. He also managed to alienate heterodox economists who saw his mathematical approach to economics with its emphasis on economic efficiency as leaving out important moral and ethical considerations.

Samuelson won the Nobel prize in economics in 1970 and went on to write one of the most influential introductory textbooks in economics. His enormous influence was felt everywhere from students just beginning their first class in economics to the highest realms of academia. Whether you're a supporter or critic of modern economics there is no denying the pivotal role that Paul Samuelson has played, for better or for worse, in the development of the economics profession.

Ostrom and Williamson win Nobel Prize

Elinor Ostrom[9] of Indiana University in Bloomington and Oliver Williamson[10] from the University of California at Berkeley won the Nobel Prize in economics in 2009 for their work on economic governance and the organization of cooperation.

The problem of managing common property is an important problem in economics. If common property is poorly managed, it can be over-exploited as a common property resource. Over-fishing or pollution of lakes and streams can be caused by poor common property management. This problem is referred to as the tragedy of the commons.

At the other extreme, common property can be unexploited or underexploited as explained by Michael Heller in his book *The Gridlock Economy.* Heller notes that joint ownership can make negotiating a contract almost impossible when each one of many owners has veto power.[11] Ostrom's research explains how common property can be managed effectively.

Ostrom's contribution is explained in detail in her 1990 book *Governing the Commons.* She noted that earlier work by economists offered three dominant models of collective behavior which are (1) the tragedy of the commons, (2) the prisoners' dilemma, and (3) the logic of collective action. These earlier models of collective behavior assume a free-rider problem where there is no trust and everyone is out for themselves. A free rider is someone who takes the benefits from common ownership without paying his or her fair share of the costs. Ostrom's work shows what happens when participants do not act as free riders but instead trust one another and cooperate to achieve a better outcome for all.

Williamson's research has included work on the difference between the way markets perform when participants act as anonymous actors versus when personal relationships are formed between producers and their suppliers. Transaction costs can be quite different depending upon how market participants relate to one another. At one extreme, market participants can be entirely unrelated dealing only in arm's length transactions. At the other extreme, transactions can take place entirely within a firm, which can substantially alter transaction costs. Again, as with Ostrom's work, Williamson research examines the role of trust and cooperation in forming and maintaining relationships.

(4.) ECONOMIC THEORY

The problems of economic governance and managing common property are important issues in economics. Ostrom and Williamson certainly deserve the Nobel prize for their insightful contributions to dealing with the role of trust and personal relationships in economics.

Economic theory must change to accommodate irrational, inconsistent and altruistic behavior

The science of economics may be profoundly changed by the failure of traditional economics to predict the recent collapse of the housing market and the freeze-up in the financial markets. For a critique of the role of economics in the financial markets, see the 2009 book *Lecturing Birds on Flying: Can Mathematical Theories Destroy the Financial Markets?* by Pablo Triana.[12]

Traditional economics is based on three key assumptions: (1) rationality, (2) consistency, and (3) self-interest. It assumes a cold, calculating, rational choice by each individual based on a stable set of preferences. It frequently doesn't work out to be that simple, because social factors intervene. The old rugged individualist, "The Marlboro Man", is a fiction.

We are all highly interdependent. Automobiles, cell phones, even breakfast cereals are created collectively. Stock market and housing bubbles are evidence of important *contagion effects*. Aliens from outer space may not see us as individuals at all, but rather as cells in a collective body that is spreading across the face of our planet. Economic theory needs drastic revision to better incorporate our collective interdependence.

Economists tried to devise methods of aggregating individual preference functions into a community-wide preference function, but finally had to accept economics Nobel prize laureate Kenneth Arrow's *Impossibility Theorem*[13] that said that under somewhat general circumstances no such aggregation of individual preferences could produce a legitimate community-wide preference function. Thus, no formal, mathematical proof has been forthcoming of Adam Smith's idea that our collective, economic well-being as a nation can be improved from each individual pursuing their own economic self-interest, as expressed in his 1776 book *An Inquiry into the Nature and Causes of the Wealth of Nations.*[14]

Instead economics detoured into *game theory* which provides many interesting results but does not solve the fundamental problem. Moreover, the outcome of any particular *game* tends to be sensitive to its own, *game*-specific assumptions. A more general economic theory is needed that is robust to a wider range of assumptions in general and allows for our collective interdependence in particular.

A good beginning for thinking about developing an economic theory of our collective interdependence is the 1976 book by Fred Hirsch called *Social Limits to Growth*[15] published by Harvard University Press.

A new branch of economics called behavioral economics tests these assumptions by performing scientific experiments to determine how people actually behave. Behavioral economists have recorded numerous situations where people do not behave rationally.

For example, advertisers have long understood that people will go to great expense to get something for "free." One professor set up an auction system that caused his students to bid more than \$20 for a \$20 bill. An irrational sense of commitment leads people to tenaciously hold on to stocks they already own, but otherwise would not be willing to purchase. These are not just trivial irregularities. In a wide-range of situations people behave irrationally from the point of view of traditional economics.

From its beginning, economics has had to fend off evidence of irrationality. *Giffen goods* that defy the law of demand by responding positively to price increases and negatively to price cuts were dismissed as special cases with little importance for overall economic policy. When some individual consumers and investors made foolish choices, economists employed the law of averages to try to reaffirm rational market outcomes. The term *rational expectations* was coined when this was extended to the behavior of monetary and fiscal policy makers.

Is it enough to simply dismiss irrationality by throwing it into the error term, or could it sometimes be the main effect? *Bounded rationality* depicts decision making in a restricted context where information is incomplete and available choices are limited. Such analysis provides the dismal science with a new basis for moving away from excessively optimistic forecasts.

The hedge fund Long Term Capital Management collapsed in 2000 when the market did not move back toward equilibrium in a reasonable amount of time. Such unexpected events are described by Nassim Taleb in his book *The Black Swan: The Impact of the Highly Improbable*.[16] Are markets ultimately efficient in the long run or is the long run just too far off? After all, it was John Maynard Keynes, the father of macroeconomics, who pointed out that "in the long run we're all dead."

The Achilles heel of traditional economics was uncovered when researchers found that irrationality is often predictable. Dan Ariely's 2008 book *Predictably Irrational* [17] is a recent popular contribution while the 2004 compendium volume *Advances in Behavioral Economics* [18] provides a more extensive coverage from the professional literature. Also see *The Paradox of Choice* [19] by Barry Schwartz, *Sway* [20] by Ori and Rom Brafman and *Free Market Madness* [21] by Peter Ubel.

Economists such as Nobel prize laureate Gary Becker led the extension of economics into the social realm in studying such things as the economics of marriage and drug addiction. Becker and his followers showed how economics can influence social behavior. The new economics is showing how social considerations can impact economics. The Nobel prize in economics was won in 2009 by Elinor Ostrom and Oliver Williamson for research that showed how organizational factors can affect economic outcomes. Social factors can have an even bigger impact on the day-to-day decisions of all of us.

For example, if you ask a friend to help you move, she may be willing to sacrifice a few of her precious Saturday hours to help out. If instead, you offer her $10 a hour to help you, she may turn you down flat. How can it make sense to be willing to work for nothing, but not be willing to do that same work for money? The answer is that social relationships are quite different from economic relationships. As soon as you make it a monetary transaction, you have changed the nature of the relationship.

An important irrational distortion occurs when a person takes possession of an item. A study randomly sorted an equal number of people into two groups. In one group each person was given a coffee mug. In the other group everyone got a candy bar. They were immediately given an opportunity to exchange the item they received for the other item. Since membership in the two groups was random, on average the ratio of people with candy bars to coffee mugs should turn out to be the same in the two groups after the final exchange. To the surprise of the researchers, the proportion of candy to mug lovers turned out to be quite different in the two groups. Each group tended to hold on to its initial gift much more than traditional economics would predict.

Decision making is more than just taking into account time and money. We also must consider the mental energy necessary to make decisions. Behavioral economists have unearthed substantial evidence of *omission bias* in economics. The stock market provides a perfect example. Researchers have found that people who own stock A which turns out to be a loser but could have purchased stock B which ultimately turns out to be a winner have much less regret than a person who initially owned stock B and then sold it to buy stock A. Even though both people end up with the losing stock A, they feel much different about it. A recent decision to hold onto a loser is not considered anywhere near as bad as the decision to buy that loser even when the monetary loss turns out to be exactly the same.

The desire to be a winner frequently distorts economic outcomes and not just when an item is offered for "free." A study offered people either $100 for sure or, alternatively, a chance to win $200 or nothing with a fifty-fifty probability. Since the expected value of the two alternative offers is the same, researchers expected about half of the people would take the $100 and the other half would try the gamble. A large proportion of the people chose the $100 with certainty. The $100 is enough to make the person a winner while the chance to get an additional $100 was not as important as the possibility of getting $0 and losing the winner status. The opposite was found when people were given a choice to lose $100 with certainty or lose $200 or $0 with a fifty-fifty probability. Most people chose the gamble since a loss of $0 was the only way to avoid being a loser. Traditional economics does not provide a mechanism for understanding such an irrational inconsistency.

George Soros allocated $50 million in October 2009 to create *The Institute for New Economic Thinking* (INET) designed to reject traditional economics. Soros's new institute will reject the efficient market theory that has performed so poorly in predicting our most recent economic recession. Soros announced his new institute in Budapest at the *Central European University*. He will fund the Institute with payments of $5 million per year for 10 years. The Institute will pay for research grants, organize conferences and create a new journal to refute the beliefs of traditional economics. An initial conference was held from April 9 through April 11, 2010, at King's College, Cambridge.

The Santa Fe Institute offers a similar venue for challenging traditional approaches to science with a multidisciplinary, nonlinear, dynamic perspective. It promotes the study of system dynamics as well as chaos and catastrophe theory. Hopefully, *The Institute for New Economic Thinking* will ultimately become just as successful.

(4.) ECONOMIC THEORY

**The next frontier in economics:
Creating markets for mental energy**

The financial crisis has exposed a deficiency in economic theory. The underlying cause of the financial crisis was the failure of individuals to exert sufficient mental energy to properly evaluate the risks involved in both the housing and financial derivatives markets. In short, people just didn't do the math.

In the housing market both, borrowers and lenders were unrealistically optimistic and failed to plan for worst-case scenarios. Likewise, purchasers of financial derivatives failed to determine exactly how much risk these financial products contained.

This problem points to a fundamental deficiency in economic theory. Traditional economics assumes that everyone has perfect information and behaves rationally in his or her own self-interest. However, a lot of irrational behavior can be explained by the limitations of the human mind. Our mental energy is limited so we follow the crowd or use rules of thumb to avoid hard thinking.

We can't treat everything as brand new every time we encounter it, so we fix expectations. We create expectations about both the physical world around us and about how the behavior of other people. We do this to conserve mental energy and avoid rethinking everything all the time. We know that others do this too. We are reluctant to challenge people's expectations. To do so is to ask them to use more of their limited supply of mental energy. We implicitly recognize that both our supply of mental energy and that of other people is limited.

There is clearly a tradeoff between time and mental energy. Students can work on their homework at a leisurely pace with the television blaring in the background, or buckle down in a quiet room and concentrate on getting the job done more quickly. Our brain uses about 25 percent of the calories consumed by our body. As we strain our brain to think, we burn up mental energy. Saying "do the math" is easy. Actually doing the math may not be so easy. Economists need to realize that not just our time and money are limited. We also have a limited supply of mental energy.

Such limits can be important. Are we better off with a president who has lots of mental energy or one who doesn't think things through carefully? It's not just being smart, but using your smarts that counts.

Economics must now be extended to take into account recent advances in medical science. Using brain scans we are now at last able to measure the amount of mental energy used in performing various tasks in terms of oxygen, electrolytes, glucose and calories consumed while looking at a pretty picture, listening to a minute of music or reading a page in a book. Once economists are able to measure something, they immediately want to create a market to buy and sell it.

Lawyers already have a market for reading all that fine print for you. They charge by the hour. Wouldn't it be more efficient to just pay for the amount of mental energy they expend? Lawyers with lots of mental energy would be able to offer people lots of good deals while those with limited mental energy not so much.

The nice thing about creating a market for mental energy is that some of it could be traded over the Internet. In effect it is already happening with some miscreants paying their fellow students to do their homework for them. Paying people for hours of routine physical labor neatly matches pay with performance. Paying people for thinking is not so neat. It would be so much more efficient if we could measure how much mental energy they are using.

How about your expenditure of mental energy at work? Maybe you should be paid by how much mental energy you expend instead of by the hour. Quick thinkers could handle a whole lot of difficult problems by lunch time and be done for the day, while slow thinkers may need to stay after hours to earn the same.

The average Wall Street banker is paid much more than the typical creative artist. We should compare the mental energy that goes into their work. Does a Wall Street banker's contribution really justify such a huge pay differential? Are labor markets really efficient or do paychecks just reflect who controls the money?

Does "Creative Capitalism" as proposed by Bill Gates make sense?

At the World Economic Forums in Davos, Switzerland, Bill Gates has promoted his pet concept of "creative capitalism" aimed at motivating companies to set aside some of their resources to help the poorest of the poor even if it reduces company profits. Does this make sense or does it distract from more efficient existing ways in which capitalism is already helping the poor?

Michael Kinsley's book *Creative Capitalism*[22] contains a wide-ranging discussion of the ideas of Bill Gates, Warren Buffett and many other corporate leaders and leading economists. It boils down to a food fight over efficient market theory. Gates suggests that the desire for *recognition* should be added to traditional profit maximization in motivating corporate behavior. Efficient-market theorists claim that brand recognition and public relations generally already incorporate recognition into the list of factors influencing business behavior. They claim that the desire for recognition is already efficiently exploited and further promotion of this motive would detract from the efficient allocation of resources.

Conservatives use the example of cell phones to demonstrate how economic inequality is self-correcting by producing a negative feedback loop that generates more benefits for the poor as the income inequality grows. They argue that initially only the rich had enough money to pay the high price of cell phones, which incorporated the high fixed costs needed to develop them. Once created, low marginal costs and intense competition drove prices down, to the benefit of poor people throughout the world. Under this theory, more income inequality just means more research to produce better products that ultimately benefit the poor. Basically this is the old trickle-down theory.

Efficient market theorists argue that capitalism is already creative and doesn't need the "improvements" offered by *Creative Capitalism*. But not all economists believe in efficient market theory. Kinsley's book retells the old joke about an economist seeing a $10 bill on the sidewalk. The economist fails to pick it up since "it couldn't be real because markets are efficient." If it were real, someone else would have already picked it up.

During the early 1990s on my way to a seminar in the Department of Economics at the University of Chicago, I noticed a $10 bill on the sidewalk along 59th street in front of Rockefeller Chapel. I looked around for the person who might have lost it and saw no one. If it had been $50, I would have reported it to the police. I figured it was unlikely that in Chicago anyone would call the cops to report the loss of $10, so I just kept it and framed it as proof that markets are not efficient.

Other authors have also argued that markets are not always efficient. In their book *A Nonrandom Walk Down Wall Street*[23] Andrew Lo and Craig MacKinlay demonstrate that there is a first mover advantage in the stock market just as there is a first mover advantage in technology improvements in any industry. Markets may be efficient given existing knowledge, but knowledge is improving all the time so markets are never perfectly efficient in this more dynamic sense. Also, new technology can fail as in the case of those financial derivatives that failed the transparency test. New knowledge is not always better knowledge or even true knowledge. Consequently, helping the poor may require going beyond traditional capitalism since unfettered markets are not always efficient.

If there is a more efficient way to help the poor, then the economy must be off of its "contract curve." As you will recall from Economics 101, the contract curve is the locus of points such that one person cannot be made better off without making someone else worse off. Such points are known to economists as *Pareto optimal* or *Pareto efficient* points. Even if there are points that are off of the contract curve and, therefore, are not Pareto optimal, the difficulty for Bill Gates and others who wish to pursue "creative capitalism" is firstly to identify such points and secondly to figure out an efficient and politically acceptable way to move to the contract curve.

Economist have long realized that there is a trade-off between maximizing the rate at which the economic pie is growing and moving toward economic equality – metaphorically known as equal pieces of our collective pie. As attempts to create socialist systems have historically shown, moving too dramatically toward income equality can cause a dramatic slowdown in the rate of increase in the size of the pie. In such a case many poor people may end up with a smaller piece of pie than they would have gotten under a system with greater inequality.

As Ralph Waldo Emerson liked to point out, usually the best position is the moderate position. Going to extremes usually just pushes the pendulum too far in one direction, leading to a colossal collapse or dramatic failure of one sort or another. In moderation Bill Gates' "creative capitalism" makes sense. The fact that it does not satisfy traditional, efficient-market theorists nor die-hard, anti-capitalist extremists is all to its credit.

Are you a socialist-creationist or a free-market evolutionist?

Is life fundamentally bottom-up and randomly designed or top-down and intentionally designed? Are biological and socio-economic systems self-organized from below or dictated from above? Free-market evolutionists see both systems as emerging from below with little help or interference from above. Socialist-creationists take the opposite position. To them the important decisions require large-scale, system-wide planning by a creator.

Are you a socialist-creationist or a free-market evolutionist? If you reject this dichotomy and instead view yourself as a socialist-evolutionist, how can you justify arguing for the power of self-organization and unintentional, benevolent design in biology and against it in economics? Are humans really autonomous decision-makers or are we following a pre-ordained path determined by our nature? Once again we are presented

(4.) ECONOMIC THEORY

with the classic nature versus nurture and self-determination debates.

In 1776 Adam Smith argued in his *Wealth of Nations* that a wide variety of high quality products did not come about through the action of governments, but rather from the industriousness of individuals. Smith's "invisible hand" did not work by the design of a benevolent creator but through the self-organizing nature of life itself. This makes sense if human evolution, including the evolution of socio-economic systems, is seem as just part of general biological evolution.

In his recent book, *The Mind of the Market*,[24] Michael Shermer points out that Smith's bottom-up vision of the world was countered in 1802 by William Paley's top-down revision in *Natural Theology* [25] where he argued that the intricacies of an eye could be the product only of a benevolent creator just as the intricacies of a watch could be the product only of a fastidious watchmaker.

In response to Paley's top-down story, Charles Darwin's 1859 book, *The Evolution of Species*,[26] explained life's self-organizing capabilities in line with Adam Smith's earlier bottom-up explanations. Life began with single-celled organisms and gradually evolved into more complex, intelligent beings. Individual ants with the right stuff self-organize their colonies for the greater good. The queen ant is not a commander ant. The colony just consists of individual ants instinctively following their nature. Clearly the socio-economic systems of ants are consistent with and dictated by their biological evolution as depicted by Darwin in *The Evolution of Species*.

The arguments of Adam Smith and Charles Darwin are linked more deeply than just their bottom-up commonality. They are bound together by a belief in the unintended nature of benevolence in both economics and evolution. Smith argued, "It is not from the benevolence of the butcher, the brewer, or the baker that we expect our dinner, but from their regard to their own interest."

Likewise, Darwin did not view "natural selection" as the result of benevolent intention, but rather as the result of random deviations in genetic code. Some deviations were beneficial and some were harmful. Those species that got the beneficial deviations prospered while those that got the harmful ones died out.

The Reverend Thomas Malthus did not share this benevolent view. His *Iron Law of Population*[27] predicted population growth would outstrip growth in the world's ability to feed its expanding population. His view that humanity was doomed to forever live in poverty on the edge of starvation gave "the dismal science" its malevolent moniker. Although he did not offer a practical solution, his dismal view of the future suggested the need for the visible hand of government to intervene.

Socialists proposed a new world order where government would control and organize production just as God was seen by some as controlling and organizing the creation of each new species.

William Paley and the socialists told a consistent, socialist-creationist story of life controlled through top-down, intentional design. Their view contrasts sharply with the free-market evolutionist story of Adam Smith and Charles Darwin who saw a world of self-organizing, bottom-up, unintentional benevolence.

5. Economic Policy: money, taxes and the minimum wage

People think of money as coins and currency. There is a lot more to it than that. Economists define money in various ways depending upon how easy it is to convert to a form that is easy to spend. Definitions of money range from very liquid to not so liquid. The M1 definition of money is the most liquid. M1 is defined as coins, currency and checking account balances. It can be used directly without having to convert it to another form. The M2 definition includes M1 but adds savings account balances.

Creating money is easy for a bank. It can take the money you deposited in your checking account and loan it out to someone else. Once the loan document is signed, the bank adds money to the borrower's checking account. Where does the bank get the money to loan out? It just takes it from your checking account. Since you and the borrower are acting as if you both had immediate access to the same money, the bank has created money by the amount of the loan. Your bank has added to the money supply. Of course, it can't do that with all of the money it receives, since it is required by law to keep some money in reserve. Also, note that the Federal Reserve can counter any money supply changes by banks through the buying and selling of treasury notes by the Federal Reserve Bank of New York in its open market operations. Ultimately, the Federal Reserve controls the money supply on a day-to-day basis in this way to keep treasury-bill interest rates within a narrow range.

The Federal Deposit Insurance Corporation (FDIC) guarantees the dollar amounts of your deposits up to a set maximum, but does not guarantee how much a dollar is worth in the economy. If inflation kicks in, the value of your money will decline. The value of money used to be guaranteed in terms of ounces of gold. Now there is no gold backing up our money. Without a guarantee it would seem to be worthless, except for the metallic value of the coins and recycled paper value of the currency. However, the government guarantees that it will accept its coins and currency as payment for taxes. Because taxes make up a big chunk of most people's paychecks, this is a quite meaningful guarantee – one that gives money real value even without the backing of gold or other precious metals.

Economics is more about using scarce resources than about claims on scarce resources that are never used. If wealthy people accumulate large sums of money that they don't use, they are not using up resources. Their excess money is just an accounting entry. If overall demand for goods and services slackens because too many rich people are not using their money, the Federal Reserve can always expand the money supply to make up the difference. Only actual consumption uses up resources, so high incomes don't mean much if the money is not used. By allowing all financial savings to be tax deferred, we would, in effect, be converting our progressive income tax into a progressive consumption tax. The IRS would not have to keep track of consumption, but only defer taxes on all savings and investments. This enhances the stability of our financial system by encouraging people to save so they can dip into their savings to maintain consumption in a recession. Switching from an income tax to a progressive consumption tax would promote savings and bolster economic security for us all.

(5.) ECONOMIC POLICY

The final selection for this chapter addresses how economists and others evaluate policy proposals. In particular we look at liberal and conservative arguments surrounding the minimum wage debate. Rigid ideology can mislead us in understanding policy issues. The minimum wage provides a perfect example of where both the left and the right can be wrong at the same time when they lock themselves into rigid policy positions.

Should California be allowed to create its own money?

During the recent recession, California reached a crisis point where it ran out of money to pay state employees. Governor Arnold Schwarzenegger and the state legislature ruled out a tax increase to pay state workers. To deal with this impasse, California issued IOUs to its employees.[1] The Bank of America[2] agreed to accept these IOUs as real money at least until July 10, 2009.[3]

Should California or any state be allowed to create its own money?[4]

Before governments got into the act, banks created money in the form of bank notes. Banks are no longer allowed to print currency for general use. Economists have longed toyed with the idea of each state printing its own money. Some people think it's the perfect solution to regional unemployment. There could be red money for Missouri, blue money for Kansas, green money for Illinois, et cetera. Each state could run its own monetary policy.

If a state like Michigan were suffering relatively more unemployment than the rest of the country, then it could just print more of its own money. It would release that money into its economy by using it to buy the bonds or other debt obligations of public or private entities within the state from state residents. That would increase the demand for goods and services in Michigan to increase employment there. Increasing the federal money supply would generate inflation in areas with low unemployment and tight supplies of goods and services. Letting the states do it instead would allow for a more targeted approach.

The problem with all this is that the American economy is highly integrated. The relatively high Michigan unemployment was largely due to the slowdown in car sales. Creating new money in Michigan is not likely to generate enough new car sales there to make a difference. Too much Michigan money would drive up the prices of other goods and services in Michigan well before it generated the number of car sales needed to re-employ all those auto workers. Furthermore, since Michigan imports many goods from other states, the excess demand is likely to bleed over to other states and drive up prices there as well. A similar explanation referencing the many specialized products that California produces would reach a similar conclusion.

The Euro Zone created in association with the European Union provides both the advantages and disadvantages of having a single currency. The Euro Zone countries have weighed the costs and benefits and have opted in while the British and Switzerland have opted out. On one hand a single currency promotes efficiency through the division and specialization of labor across countries by greasing the wheels of trade. On the other hand a single monetary authority reduces flexibility in responding to differences in national unemployment levels. If a member country and its people are profligate, they can undermine the value of the Euro. Greece has provided an example of this problem. Other EU countries felt compelled to come to Greece's aid in its financial crisis since the poor credit ratings on Greece's debt threatened to undermine the value of the Euro.

California has not behaved like Greece. Its bond ratings are similar to those of other states. Creating a separate currency for California would introduce a fluctuating exchange rate between California's currency and that of the rest of the country. This could significantly inhibit trade between California and the other states.

Unless California wants to break away from the Union and become a separate country, it should back away from creating its own money. Our founding fathers were wise enough to specify in our constitution that only the federal government is authorized to print and circulate currency. However issuing official currency is just one aspect of one way of creating money and expanding the money supply as we will see in the next commentary.

Without taxes money would have no value

Ever since we dropped the gold standard, the value of our money has been based on the government's promise to pay what? Nothing. Without taxes, our money would have no value. Money is essentially an IOU – some guy's promise to pay you back some day. If you believe you will actually get paid back, then you might accept that promise. Do we really trust the government or its money?

Creating money puts unused resources to work (or causes inflation if there are no unused resources). A pig farmer might give a corn farmer an IOU for corn so the pig farmer can raise pigs. If that corn, to be paid back at harvest time, would otherwise sit idle, then the IOU is acting like money to stimulate the economy. Of course, a store of value is just one of several roles money can play. Medium of exchange and unit of account are others.

Banks took the lead in creating money. They issued promissory notes often payable upon demand. Depositors whose banks issue IOUs still have immediate access to their money even though the bank could not pay if all depositors demanded their money. To the extent that the depositor doesn't withdraw the money during the period of the loan, the bank's IOU increases the demand for goods and services in the economy. Then governments got into the act of creating money. Initially they issued coins that had at least some intrinsic value, but soon backed their currencies with a promise to pay in gold or, in some cases, in silver.

Ultimately many governments abandoned the promise to pay in gold or silver, and, instead, created what is known to economists as "fiat" money. Basically "fiat" money nominally has value just because the government says it does. In theory, "fiat" money should be worthless.[5] Who is going to believe the government, or worse yet, the politicians who control the government? The real reason that money has value is because you have to pay your taxes in money. Pay up or go to jail.

Bernanke versus Geithner: their roles for credit or blame

Time Magazine chose Ben Bernanke for its *Person of the Year* for 2009.[6] Why not Tim Geithner? Should the Senate have renewed Bernanke? Should Geithner be removed?[7]

These questions require a clear understanding of the roles of the Fed versus the Treasury. Who is the real hero or villain in the running of our economy? Who wields the power of the purse? Did *Time* miss the mark by naming Bernanke instead of Geithner? We need to review the two quite different roles played by these two men in their jobs as Fed chief and Treasury chief, respectively.

The Treasury prints the money but the Federal Reserve creates it. What does that mean? It means that the Treasury prints the money but can give it only to the Federal Reserve Banks, which distribute the cash to private banks that request it in return for debiting their accounts with the Fed. The Federal Reserve creates money by buying treasury bills (a kind of government bond) in the New York money market and crediting the accounts of the sellers with dollar amounts. In doing so it expands the money supply.*

Bernanke has the authority to create money while Geithner does not. If Geithner wants to spend more money than the Treasury has collected, he has to borrow it by selling treasury bills in the New York money market. It is up to Bernanke to decide whether to finance Geithner's deficit spending by buying up those treasury bills or not. If so, the new money that Bernanke provides in the form of bank credits will keep interest rates down.

---

* *Actually anyone can attempt to expand the money supply, but the Fed controls the money supply by maintaining a target interest rate for treasury bills in the New York money market by buying and selling treasury bills as needed to keep close to that target. In effect, the Fed acts to counter any attempt to increase or decrease the money supply. If you take $100 out of your mattress and put it in a checking account, the bank may loan out some of that money which would tend to expand the money supply if the Fed did not counter it. The money supply expands when banks loan money that you and the borrower both think is available to spend at the same time.*

If not, then Geithner must sell his treasury bills to others including foreigners such as the Chinese, who have financed a lot of our debt in recent years.

Without Bernanke providing new money, Geithner will have to offer higher interest rates to sell additional treasury bills in the financial market. The more treasury bills Geithner tries to sell, the higher interest rates will go. Higher rates slow our economy by choking off private borrowing by both businesses and individuals. So far Bernanke has been keeping interest rates low by buying up Geithner's treasury bills.

During times of high unemployment the additional money that Bernanke provides will allow business to expand production and consumers to expand their demand for products. Geithner played his part by financing government spending in excess of revenues, but Bernanke has the final say on the short term impact of the deficit on the economy.

However, if we were at full employment, then Bernanke's purchase of Geithner's treasury bills would put too much money into our economy. Too much money chasing too few products causes inflation.

Conservatives criticize both Geithner and Bernanke for their roles in expanding government's role in the economy. They argue that when business borrows money, it uses it to produce more products, but the government just spends borrowed money without producing more goods. More spending without producing more products means more inflation.

Liberals point out that the government provides many services. Inflation only occurs when too much money is chasing too few goods *and* services. They also note that Geithner running a deficit and Bernanke expanding the money supply together help stimulate the economy in times of high unemployment.

Both Bernanke and Geithner have been creative in coming up with various financial incentives to get our economy back on track. Bernanke has been at it longer and his decisions under current law are independent of the Congress and the President. Geithner operates under the direction of the President with Congressional approval of his budget.

At the end of the day I would say that *Time Magazine* is right on. Bernanke has played a greater independent role in this whole mess for better or for worse. Let's hope that history finds his decisions to be right on for the health of our economy as well.

Enhance financial security, cut income taxes with tax-deferred savings plan

Greed reveals itself not in income but in consumption. Warren Buffett has lived in the same modest house since 1958,[8] but other wealthy people live in enormous houses costing tens of millions of dollars. Many famous people have just one or two homes and just a few vehicles while others spend lavishly on many homes and dozens of cars.[9]

It really doesn't hurt for people to have bank account balances with lots of digits. Even if they hoard money in mattresses, the Fed can increase the money supply appropriately to match our economy's potential for producing goods and services. If accumulating tons of money motivates some and feeds their egos, that's fine. It's only when they use that money to make extravagant purchases, driving up prices and taking resources away from the rest of us, that it really matters.

Saving money has lots of advantages for both the individual and our economy as a whole. If people keep lots of money stashed away for a rainy day, it will help even out the ups and downs of our economy. When people lose their jobs or have unexpected medical expenses, having a hoard of cash can ease the financial pain and help keep the economy on a more even keel.

Aside from destroying your money, losing it or giving it away, there are two main things you can do with your income: spend it or save it. What if we taxed only what we spend? How could we do this without placing an excessive burden on poor people who spend a much higher proportion of their income than rich people?

The answer is to stop taxing savings and turn our progressive income tax into a progressive consumption tax.[10] All direct deposits from your employer to your saving or investment accounts would be tax deferred. Withdrawals from saving or investment accounts would be taxed. In effect, that would convert our income tax into a consumption tax without having to keep track of actual consumption. We want to discourage excessive individual consumption while maintaining strong aggregate consumption and savings. The ideal consumption tax would have zero or very low tax rates for modest consumption and progressively higher rates as consumption reaches excessive levels.

This would require adjusting fiscal and monetary policies simultaneously. In fiscal policy we could allow all interest income and direct-deposited income as well as self-employed income deposited within 60 days to be tax-deferred. In monetary policy, we could increase the money supply slightly to take up the slack as people respond to the incentive to save more money and spend less. The increased money supply will drive down interest rates making business investment easier, thus helping maintain strong demand for our economy's goods and services.

We all need to save more money for retirement and for all those medical expenses in our golden years that might not be fully covered by our health insurance. Since most medical costs occur toward the end of life, saving more money now for use later on makes lots of sense. Our tax laws need to be changed to reflect these realities. In the long run our economy will be healthier and so will we.

Conservatives and liberals oversimplify analysis of minimum wage

Don't buy in to all that left wing and right wing ideology. Right wing extremists use oversimplified logic with analogies that really don't hold up very well. Left wing extremists are just conformist members of a social club committed to a preconceived set of conclusions. Both groups don't have to think too hard, but just manipulate the evidence to support their ideology with its well-defined policy positions.

It doesn't matter how smart someone is if they are not willing to invest time and mental energy in crafting effective policies. A good leader ignores partisan ideology and finds practical solutions to our problems.

For example, what is the effect of the minimum wage on fast-food restaurants? Right wingers claim that it just forces prices higher and causes the restaurants to reduce the number of labor hours of employment.[11] Left wingers claim it helps those most marginal in society, the working poor.[12]

Economists pursuing such matters with objective research have discovered some evidence that both sides are wrong. It appears that raising the minimum wage by the amounts historically observed causes new workers to apply for fast-food jobs. These workers tend to be more productive workers such as a retiree, a house-spouse or a college student on vacation. They show up for work on time, are more productive on the job, and treat customers better than some of the marginal workers who are the only ones willing to take such jobs when the pay is lower.

Because restaurants can count on their new workers, they don't have to overstaff positions. Along with greater productivity, this saves money. The new workers enhance customer relations, which increases business. Consequently, restaurants are not forced to raise prices nor cut labor hours. Historically, there is no strong evidence to show a significant reduction in employment or undue inflationary pressure caused by increasing the minimum wage.

Just as right wingers are sometimes wrong, left wingers are sometimes wrong too. Are the working poor being crowded out of jobs now paying more under a higher minimum wage? Do left-wing policies sometimes end up hurting the very people they are trying to help? Empirical evidence is key.

From time-to-time reasonable increases in the minimum wage may sometimes be a good thing. Additional studies may present new evidence which may alter conclusions, but that's the point. Right wing extremists and left wing extremists don't really care about the evidence. They know where they stand and have no intention of letting the facts get in their way.

Both sides treat politics as if it were some sort of religion. They are the Hutus and Tutsis of America, bitterly sticking to their policy "guns" and clinging to their political "religions." Let's hope moderates prevail.

6. Research Methods:
system dynamics forecasting, issues with randomized trials

To the uninitiated, statistical studies seem complicated enough already. However, much more work is needed in both economics (econometrics) and medical studies (epidemiology) to properly control for the complex interrelationships that affect our finances and our health.

Theory plays a central role in the scientific method. Without a proper theory we are slaves to the latest roll of the dice. Just as there are statistical relationships in the population we are studying, those same statistical relationships can be expected to exist in a sample from that population. Unfortunately, there are other relationships in the sample that are unique to that sample and do not reflect any corresponding population relationships. Without theory we are tricked into thinking the relationships we observe in the latest sample are true for all time in time series studies or for all cross-sectional units (e.g. people) in cross sectional studies. Evidence would never accumulate because the reported relationships would change constantly from study to study. A properly developed theory with testable hypotheses enables us to avoid such pitfalls and zero in on relationships that hold up sample after sample. Those are most likely the population relationships being sampled by the data generating process. This is the scientific method.

Often in any given study there is an explanatory variable of interest and a dependent variable thought to be influenced by that explanatory variable. But the effect of age on income or smoking on heart disease cannot be properly determined without controlling for other confounding factors such as education and exercise, respectively. These additional control variables stand at the heart of any proper theory. Economics (and physics) have quite elaborate theories involving a host of control variables. Theory in medicine is, by contrast, almost nonexistent. Little, if any, theory exists about the rather important relationship in our bodies between the electrical system and the chemical system, or between our digestive and circulatory systems. However, at the very least medical studies should include known or suspected control variables wherever and whenever possible.

Economists have developed many complex structural and behavioral theories about economic relationships but dropped the ball when attempting to forecast such systems. Instead of including all of the complex interrelationships into their models, they tended to shift to purely time series analysis models which dropped such relationships in favor of complex statistical analyses. Economics must now go back and pick up those well-developed theoretical relationships and incorporate them into their models in the form of system dynamics models which are capable of retaining the structural and behavioral relationships while projecting the time dynamics for forecasting. It is time to test all those testable hypotheses in a system dynamics context.

Econometrics and epidemiology need to get their acts together and finally face the more complex interrelationships that better represent reality than those oversimplified and erroneous models they have been attempting to pass off as important scientific research.

Research needed to end economy's boom-bust cycle

Conservatives are correct in identifying government as a contributor to our economy's boom-bust cycle,[1] but liberals are right in seeing an important role for government.

Economists generally agree that interest rates and the money supply play an important role in our economy. Conservatives emphasize the importance of interest rates in allocating resources between the present and the future. Since the economy has a fixed amount of resources at any given time, some mechanism must determine what proportion of those resources should be used for consumption now and what proportion should go to investment to allow for increased consumption in the future.

When consumers are determined to consume as much as possible right now, they will save very little. Consequently, little money will be available for companies to borrow. Just as farmers borrow money to plant a bigger crop now and pay off the loan at harvest time, companies borrow money to develop new and better products for the future. Companies that want to borrow will compete for what little savings are available and drive up interest rates, which will curtail investment. The interest rate is the price of borrowing money. That price gets high when people save very little. Consume now and forget the future.

If consumers change their minds and want to save more now for future consumption, such as in retirement, they will provide the financial markets with more savings that will bring down the price of money, which is the interest rate. A lower interest rate will allow companies to borrow more now to expand their investment activities.

So far, so good. Interest rates play a key role in allocating resources between the present and future, but what happens when government intervenes? If the Federal Reserve expands the money supply when the economy is already at full employment, then it will be implying that we can have our cake and eat it too. Increasing the money supply brings down interest rates without the necessity of people saving more. We can consume more now and consume more in the future too. Only we can't. Resources are limited. We really can't have our cake and eat it too. The increased demand for resources for both consumption and investment will drive up the prices of those resources to begin an inflationary spiral.

But what if our resources are not being fully used such as in a recession? In that situation it makes sense for the Fed to maintain a higher than normal money supply to keep interest rates low to encourage both consumption and investment at the same time. However, conservatives cite past experience that the Fed doesn't know when to take its foot off the gas and stop pumping up our economy.

Excessive expansion will just lead us into another boom to be followed by another inevitable bust. What is the real problem here and what is the solution? The real problem is that neither government nor business has yet developed accurate forecasting mechanisms that adequately take into account the positive and negative feedback loops and time delays in tracking the economy's future path. Nor do these models sufficiently incorporate the prospect of predictably irrational behavior by investtors and consumers. A lot more work needs to be done on developing appropriate statistical forecasting methods.

Conservative such as Milton Friedman gave up on this quest a long time ago and recommended that the Fed just expand the money supply at a constant rate of about two or three percent a year to keep up with the natural, long-term expansion of our economy.[2]

The econometric methods that are currently being used for forecasting are not adequate. Models that incorporate the structural and behavioral relationships between money supply and interest rates, consumer demand and employment, and our exports and imports require new estimates on a month-by-month basis, which are not forthcoming from most of our current structural and behavioral models.

Instead, economists have borrowed and developed time series models from the statistical profession which track a few sets of variables as their values twist and turn in complex patterns over time, but without taking into account all the known structural and behavioral relationships among the multitude of variables that drive our economy. What we need are models that combine known structural and behavioral relationships with the complex dynamics of statistical time series models.

The most promising methodology is called "system dynamics." System dynamics[3] provides a framework for developing models that treat all variables except time itself as being *endogenous,* which means they are determined within the system and are not *exogenous,* which means coming from outside of the system.[4] Such models can combine the structural and behavioral relationships with the complex time dynamics that can better enable the Fed to know when to begin to slowly contract the money supply to raise interest rates and bring our economy to a soft landing at essentially full employment levels.

Conservatives and liberals may disagree philosophically about the role of government and business, but at the end of the day what most Americans care about is what works to restore jobs while fending off inflation that eats away our retirement savings.

Remember it took the Wright brothers a while to figure out how to control an airplane.[5] It took even longer to develop planes that could carry heavy loads at great speeds over long distances, not to mention the moon landings and our missions to Mars.[6]

With sufficient effort and determination we will master the art of controlling our economy. For the sake of both our retired citizens on fixed incomes and our long-term jobless citizens, let's accomplish this soon.

Problems in business and economic analysis

In a speech in Kansas City, Federal Reserve Chairman Ben Bernanke defended bank bailouts, saying he stopped a second Great Depression, and called for Congress to create new ways to handle future large bank failures. However, he didn't get at the source of the problem: systemic flaws that cause failures in business strategies and economic analysis.

Each business must evaluate its risks and rewards, but it should never take the economy's course and speed for granted. It is critical to evaluate both U.S. and international sources of risk, not just for your own business and the immediate market, but for the economy as a whole.

Just as businesses make the mistake of taking the economy's course and speed for granted, government and academic economists take business rationality and efficiency for granted. *Efficient market theory*[7] assumes that the price of a product or service already takes into account all available information about all possible risks and rewards.

For way too long, too many businesses have operated under the assumption that current economic conditions will continue to prevail. Should you take more risk to go for that extra buck, or prepare for the worst so that you will survive while your competitors die when the worst happens?

Business economists tend to assume that the overall economy will always operate efficiently. They focus on how to avoid their company's own mistakes and possible inefficiencies. Academic economists assume just the opposite. They assume that individual businesses will always operate efficiently (e.g. a monopoly will always efficiently maximize its profits) but the system as a whole may develop problems from mistaken government policies or exogenous perturbations such as crop failures.

At Milton Friedman's 90th birthday party in 2002 at the University of Chicago, Ben Bernanke was the main speaker.[8] That was when he gave his famous admission that the Federal Reserve holds substantial responsibility for prolonging the Great Depression. Now is the time to admit that economics has failed us in its ability to accurately forecast the future path of our economy and the impact of monetary policy.

Masters and Ph.D. programs in economics must now face the fact that markets are not perfect and can go into disequilibrium for extended periods with cataclysmic outcomes. In particular all economists must become sensitized to *contagion effects*[9] where correlated behavior drastically increases risks. Business should not just ask "Will I make more money if I do this?" but also "What if everyone does this?".

Running worst-case simulations must now become standard practice for both business and government economists. We must pay more attention to places like *The Santa Fe Institute** which specializes in studying dynamic, nonlinear systems. Academic economists must train their MBA students and Ph.D. candidates in system dynamics.

System dynamics is key to success in economic forecasting

When is the worst over? When is it time to jump back into the stock market? Economic models will fail to tell us where our economy is going unless they incorporate system dynamics.

Traditionally economic models have consisted of a number of equations that logically explain how the various sectors of the economy interact with one another. The money supply affects interest rates, which are inversely related to bond prices. Wages and salaries affect consumer demand, which affects output and, ultimately, employment and inflation.

To use these models for forecasting, they must allow past values to predict future values. This means introducing lagged variables. A lagged variable is one whose value predicts either its future value or the future value of another variable. This works fine for describing the past where the lagged values are all known such as when you want to predict just one period ahead as traditional models do. But what if you want to forecast the state of the economy many periods into the future?

* www.santafe.edu

(6.) RESEARCH METHODS

The problem is that the future values of the lagged variables are generally unknown. The "solution" that economists have come up with is to use so-called "time series" models which express the value of a variable such as stock prices as a function of its past values. In other words, you get next period's predicted values on the basis of last period's predicted values. The problem is that the time series models lack much of the intuitive, logical relationships of the traditional economic models.

The real solution to this problem has been largely ignored by economists. Engineers at MIT and elsewhere have developed models that are much better equipped to deal with the interrelationships involved in forecasting. Their system dynamics models are basically systems of differential equations with positive and negative feedback loops and time delays. These models allow for both the traditional logical and intuitive economic relationships and an effective way of forecasting their values.

The reason that economists have eschewed system dynamics models is that their statistical properties have been difficult to determine. They could produce biased and inconsistent estimates. They also quickly turn into a rather complex system of equations that become impossible to solve analytically. Fortunately, there are now many efficient methods that can solve large systems of differential equations numerically instead.

System dynamics models work well in forecasting because they extend the traditional economics models to explain all values of all variables *within the model* except for the value of *time* itself, which, of course, is already known infinitely into the future. In statistical lingo, this is to say that all values in a system dynamics model are "endogenous" (determined within the system) except for time which is "exogenous" (determined outside of the system).** Traditional economics models contain one or more exogenous variables besides time. The time series models leave out the traditional economic inter-relationships so important to economic analysis. System dynamics models solve both of these problems.

Until rather recently, economists also rejected so-called "nonparametric" models that build themselves. Ironically, nonparametric models often end up having more parameters than their parametric counterparts. With nonparametric models, you never know how many parameters you are going to have until you complete the estimation process. The old "stepwise regression" models are nonparametric models that allow a variable to be tried on for fit before deciding whether to include it or not.[10] These models were rejected because they could not be shown to produce unbiased and consistent estimates.

Advances in asymptotic analysis have allowed the determination of statistical properties for many nonparametric models when large data samples and high-powered computers are available. Consequently, nonparametric methods are becoming popular in economics.[11]

Advanced asymptotic analysis[12] should now be used to validate system dynamics models for forecasting in economics. This has already been demonstrated for some system dynamics models. If there were ever a time when we needed to be able to peer into the crystal ball and foretell our economic future, now would be it. System dynamics models can show the way. Free system dynamics software is available from Vensim.[13] MATLAB has an extension called "Simulink" for creating and running system dynamics models.[14] Dynamo, Powersim, STELLA and iThink also offer system dynamics software.

** http://en.wikipedia.org/wiki/Exogeny

Control variables needed in randomized trials

An old joke defines a *statistician* as a person who can put one hand in boiling water and the other hand in freezing water and say "On average I feel just fine." Getting FDA approval requires presenting convincing evidence that a drug or procedure is effective for the *average* patient and not dangerous for the vast majority of patients.[15] The problem is that the average patient may not exist at all. Even when such a patient does exist, that Jill or Joe Average might not be you.

The aim of a great deal of medical research is to get approval from the FDA for some drug or medical procedure. Other considerations such as determining the drug's or procedure's appropriateness for individuals are often ignored or "left for future research" and never done. Health could be improved, and vast sums of money saved, if the research were done correctly and completely.

To avoid systematic bias in medical studies, patients are randomly and secretly assigned to a *treatment* group to take the real drug or a *control* group to take a placebo drug that looks real but is really just a dummy drug that does nothing.[16] The best of such randomized studies are *double-blind* which means that neither the doctor administering the treatment nor the patient knows if the drug is real or a placebo.[17]

It is not possible to carry out a randomized trial when the treatment cannot be randomly assigned.[18] For example, it is not feasible to randomly assign some people to be smokers and others to be nonsmokers. In that case an observational study is done instead. Systematic bias could distort the results if nonsmokers were more likely to work out at the gym or eat more healthful food than smokers. Consequently, observational studies require including a host of *control variables* such as age, gender, exercise and nutrition to extract out their effect on your probability of getting cancer. This is important because your chances of getting cancer might be quite different from that of Jill or Joe Average.

Including control variables also allows researchers to check for interaction effects. For example, the effect of age on the probability of a heart attack or stroke depends on a person's gender. A drug that might be very important for a man might be less important for a pre-menopausal woman of the same age. In other words the effect of age cannot be determined in isolation; gender and other factors may be important in finding out the impact of age on heart attacks.

Randomized clinical trials are considered the gold standard of medical research, but, more often than not, they are used to avoid determining the effect of a drug or procedure on an individual patient. Analyses of randomized trials typically don't bother with control variables. Since patients are randomly assigned to their groups, the average values of the control variables tend to be more or less the same for the two groups. For purposes of convincing the FDA to accept the drug, the researchers can claim a balanced study that not only uses two groups with equal observable characteristics but presumably has equal unobservable or unknown characteristics as well.

Why bother with control variables in a randomized clinical trial? Two reasons that have nothing to do with FDA approval jump out at you immediately. First, each individual can get much more appropriate and effective treatment if control variables are used to determine the effect of the drug or procedure on them as individuals. Second, lots of money can be saved if drugs and procedures are just used on people who are helped by them and not by people on whom they are ineffective.

Not all medical studies are done poorly. At a research presentation sponsored by the Biostatistics Department at the University of Kansas Medical Center in Kansas City.[19] Professor Seng-jaw Soong[20] gave a talk "Multivariate Modeling of Melanoma Prognosis and its Web-based Applications." His study was a randomized clinical trial. He not only included important control variables, but he also checked for interaction effects among the variables.[21] To make sure that the results of his work would be used appropriately for individuals, he created a website where you can plug in your personal characteristics to get results that are appropriate for you as an individual and not just for Jill or Joe Average.

The FDA should change the rules of the game. Not only should new drugs and procedures have to be effective for the average patient and be harmless for the vast majority of patients, but control variables must be included and a website must be created where patients and their doctors can check the appropriateness of the drug or procedure for that specific patient. Checking for interaction effects must be part of the analysis.

It is time to stop one-size-fits-all medicine. Write to Congress to demand that the FDA wake up to its responsibilities to individual Americans and stop wasting our lives and our money.

BRAIN ON FIRE

7. Foreign Affairs:
Africa, foreign aid and China

U nfortunately, too much of the foreign aid sent to
Africa is controlled by corrupt government officials
who demand bribes and payoffs. This top-down
organization and control generally discourage and often
block business development at the bottom. Friends, clans
and tribes of top officials benefit on the basis of their
connections instead of their competitive efficiency and
productivity. The focus in countries where aid and natural
resource wealth is controlled by government officials is on
dividing up the economic pie rather than enlarging it. The
first selection in this chapter reviews Dambisa Moyo's
book *Dead Aid*, which explains how foreign aid and
natural resource wealth can prevent a country from
escaping from poverty.[1]

Too often economists view economic development as
the problem of organizing an economy to maximize a
country's gross domestic product (GDP). This top-down
view ignores the source of wealth creation. Nature takes
an entirely different approach. The classic example is the
ant colony. The queen ant does not hand down orders
from above. Instead ants react to stimuli in their
immediate surroundings to instinctively organize
themselves with great efficiency at the local level.
Successful economies operate in much the same way.
Encouraging local businesses to flourish is essential for
maximizing the creativity and productivity of each
person. Even in the largest, most developed economies,
most workers are employed by small businesses or are
self-employed. Only a small portion work for large

119

enterprises. The second selection discusses this problem as discussed in a related book by Glenn Hubbard and William Duggan called *The Aid Trap*.[2]

China has been moving quickly to establish itself as a key economic player in the 21st century. The economies of China and the United States are already becoming highly integrated. American officials complain that China is manipulating its currency to sell its products to American consumers at excessively low prices. Many of the cheap products that China produces are no longer made in America. Although the low quality tires sold at Wal-Mart and other discount retailers are no longer produced in the United States, President Obama has insisted on imposing a temporary tariff on such tires to avoid disrupting such tire production.[3] In a sense all this is reminiscent of what happened in Japan right after World War II. Japanese companies exported a torrent of cheap products to the United States. The term "made in Japan" was used to refer to any cheap and useless product. The Japanese were insulted so they switched gears and with the advice of American quality control expert Edwards Deming, they created a host of high-quality automotive and electronic products. Now history is repeating itself with China. Cheap product production is moving on to Vietnam and other low-wage countries as China moves on to produce higher quality products.

The other highly contentious issue with China is democracy. People naturally tend to feel more secure when their friends look and act just like them – remember that clique of giggly girls in high school? America is no different. We would sure feel more secure if China were a democracy. In this chapter we discuss the difference between external freedom (freedom from foreign domination) and internal freedom (democracy).

(7.) FOREIGN AFFAIRS

Throughout history people have sacrificed internal freedom in order to secure their external freedom. With China's history of being exploited by foreign powers as well as internal turmoil, we should not be surprised by its reluctance to loosen up its central controls. As with Iran, the best policy may be to indirectly encourage those favoring democracy while avoiding any appearance of interfering with internal affairs.[4]

The section on Kiva.org[5] is designed to point out how the Internet now frees each citizen to establish their own "foreign policy" by directly loaning money to individuals starting or expanding businesses in developing countries or, now, in low-income areas in the United States itself. One way to reduce the number of mischief makers around the world is to keep everyone busy with business. Surely, getting rich is more fun than blowing yourself up in a suicide bombing.

Has 50 years of U.S. AID money stymied African growth?

In her 2009 book *Dead Aid* [6] Oxford Ph.D. economist Dambisa Moyo argues that foreign aid to Africa has not just been ineffective, but has actually blocked African economic development. Are we not only throwing U.S. taxpayer money down the drain but also hurting Africans in the process?

In recent years economists have become increasingly aware that natural resources, especially oil resources, can be a curse on a country rather than a blessing. Foreign money must first be exchanged for local currency before it can buy local goods. Large purchases of the local currency can drive up its price in the

121

international foreign exchange markets. Foreign money seeking to purchase a nation's oil can drive up the value of the local currency to the point that its products become too expensive to sell in international markets. Moyo points out that this problem, which is known to economists as the *Dutch disease*,[7] can also be caused by foreign aid money pouring into an economy.

The Economist came up with the term *Dutch disease* to describe the deterioration of the manufacturing sector in the Netherlands after a large natural gas field was developed there with the help of foreign oil companies. Examples of countries affected by the *Dutch disease* outside of Africa include Venezuela and Iran. Some African countries with oil, gold or diamonds have been subject to a double whammy of the natural resource curse and foreign aid dependency.

Foreign aid not only drives up the value of the local currency to block the country's export growth, but frequently is tied to the required purchase of donor country commodities, such as U.S. grain, to further drive a nail in the coffin of the country's economy by displacing local grain farmers.

Moyo notes that the well-intentioned donation of $1-million worth of mosquito netting provided immediate medical benefits but destroyed a nascent mosquito net industry that employed many Africans. Moreover, destroying the netting industry eliminated the source of replacement netting which will be needed when the donated netting eventually wears out and falls apart.

In a poor, democratic country without natural resources or foreign aid, people determined to become rich do not go into government. When a democratic government has no money except the little it can collect from its poor citizens, politicians make a personal sacrifice by going into politics where they generally make a lot less money than in the private sector. Moreover, the people demand that the money be spent to their benefit and not be squandered. (With no natural resources or foreign aid, the primary way to increase a country's wealth is to build the country's human capital by educating its people.)

Conversely, when the money arrives top-down instead of emerging from bottom up, corrupt politicians have first crack at the money and can dispose of the rest as patronage for their supporters. Controlling the money means controlling the voters instead of the other way around. We have recently seen this problem develop in Afghanistan where foreign aid money has been misdirected by corrupt officials. Corruption in Haiti blocked distribution of much-needed, emergency medical supplies from the Port-au-Prince airport following the earthquake there until the media got wind of the story.[8]

Moyo reviews other explanations for the poor economic performance of many African countries and essentially shows them to be symptoms rather than the cause of the problem. Ultimately she argues that foreign aid fosters dependency similar to welfare dependency. Until African countries have to stand on their own two feet, they will never attain economic maturity. Her recommendations include gradually weaning Africa off of foreign aid and removing obstacles such as agricultural subsidies in donor countries that unfairly undermine African economic development.

Can free markets and local businesses convert poverty into prosperity when foreign aid fails?

The World Bank's annual report, *Doing Business*, ranks countries on the basis of how easy it is to start and run a business. In their book *The Aid Trap*[9] professors Glenn Hubbard and William Duggan point out that countries that rank high in *Doing Business* have more prosperity and much less poverty than countries that rank low.[10] They review the unlikely emergence of prosperity in modern times after millennia of humans struggling for survival where poverty was a welcomed alternative to the only other common outcome – early death. The business system was suppressed throughout history by other competing systems such as the tribal, despotic, feudal, national socialist and pure socialist systems. At first the business system developed only in isolated pockets where the anti-business forces were weak such as in Venice in Southern Europe and Amsterdam in Northern Europe. From there business spread in fits and starts ultimately to London and Manchester in England and beyond.

Economics got its moniker of the dismal science when economists in general, and David Riccardo[11] in particular, foresaw nothing but continued poverty with population growth exceeding economic growth even as the industrial revolution began. Adam Smith,[12] on the other hand, got the point early on. Free enterprise invokes the division and specialization of labor to enhance productivity, allowing substantial numbers of people to escape the poverty trap. Falling birth rates in England as per capita incomes rose created a virtuous circle in the form of a positive feedback loop. Greater productivity generated higher economic growth rates which in turn drove down population growth rates. As child labor became less important to family survival, families had fewer children. A similar story has played out in other developed nations and is playing out today in the emerging market countries.

Just as the power of ideas can liberate a people from poverty, such power can enslave them. We are still suffering from the misconceptions of some baby boomers throughout the world. In the eyes of some people, the post World War II Soviet Union was a progressive society seeking justice and prosperity for its least advantaged citizens. In their formative years, some people embraced the Soviet story of fairness and equality along with its short-term technological achievements. Western countries that today are relatively pro-business gave aid to anti-business, non-aligned socialist countries after the Soviet Union proved its system superior by winning the 1960 Olympics.[13] Their goal was to prevent the non-aligned countries from joining the Soviet countries in the growing anti-Western alliance of socialist countries. The success of the Soviet *sputnik* (satellite)[14] and related feats of technological prowess deceived many westerners into thinking that the Soviet way was the wave of the future.

In Africa the pro-socialist mindset among older Africans is still evident. For some people, free enterprise is still seen as just a vestige of foreign domination and imperialist exploitation. It is no surprise that they have welcomed China's investments, which come with China's policy of no interference in a nation's internal affairs. Moreover, China itself was also a victim of the imperialist powers. Westerners promoting business enterprise as the only true path to prosperity are viewed with suspicion by some older leaders who see their own power threatened by the unfettered expansion of the business class.

After World War II, Britain and France voted in leadership that was wary of returning to unfettered capitalism because of the economic suffering between the two world wars. They were somewhat sympathetic to socialist ideals and turned over key industries to government ownership or oversight. Nobel prize winning economists tended to be honored for work that was applicable to both capitalism and socialism.

From the point of view of national and international aid agencies as well as private non-governmental aid organizations (NGOs), it was much easier to distribute aid money to national socialist governments with five-year plans than to try to figure out how to distribute money and other resources directly to people in need within those countries. Even where aid resources were not diverted, corruption in high places ensured that government officials receiving aid money could obtain bribes and payoffs for its distribution.

Hubbard and Duggan note that the Marshall plan has been commonly misunderstood in that it provided aid to businesses much more directly than most people realize. The mistaken belief that the Marshall plan just provided relief supplies and built roads, bridges, ports and other infrastructure is well-established in some people's minds. In fact, Hubbard and Duggan argue that the funds from the Marshall plan were given first to local businesses. When the businesses succeeded and paid back the loans to local governments, those governments, in turn, then used the funds to build infrastructure. The professors argue that European revival was more a matter of developing businesses first and adding infrastructure later. Without an expanding local business sector the revival of Western Europe as a stalwart for democracy in fending off the Russians may well have been a failure. Lifting Europe out of poverty was due primarily to the revival of business.

In *The Aid Trap* the authors offer local business development under free enterprise as an alternative to pure socialism and national socialism. They propose an Economic Cooperation Administration (ECA) to promote local businesses in a manner similar to the Marshall plan. Freeing Africa from poverty can only come about by freeing businesses from the undue burdens of excessive taxation and regulation with accompanying corruption requiring a myriad of bribes and payoffs. When local businesses are free to grow, Africa can finally follow the developed countries and emerging nations out of poverty.

To promote capitalism and enhance our soft power, go to Kiva.org

Our rich, cultural diversity provides us with the enormous potential to use our soft power to influence the world. Our uniquely diverse country has an African component that can speak convincingly to Africans, a Latin component that can speak convincingly to Latin Americans, an Asian component that can speak convincingly to Asians, a European component that can speak convincingly to Europeans, et cetera. Yet within our borders, we speak freely to one another without the intense cultural isolationism, hostility and antagonisms that are so often evident elsewhere in the world.

For better or for worse, humans have always been more trusting of members of their own clan or tribe. America is the clan of clans and tribe of tribes. Our diversity empowers us to bridge the gaps and great divides among the nations of the world. It is not just our military might that sets us apart but our inclusiveness. To use an old cliché: "We are them and they are us."

In some respects we provide a mirror image of the world that wets the appetite of our young people to learn more. We have never had a generation more eager to explore the world than our younger generation. Still in their 20s they are often considerably more traveled than their parents and grandparents. In contrast to previous generations, they are much more likely to have an ethnically diverse set of friends. In this respect, we are different from much of the rest of the world, which largely remains ethnically divided.

In an attempt to bridge this divide, the European Union (EU) has demonstrated the enormous economic and cultural benefits of bringing together a diversity of cultures and languages, not to subsume them, but to celebrate them. We should appreciate the value of this approach and take the lead in bringing the world together.

In economics you can do this by going to www.kiva.org and loaning a small (or large) bit of money to the budding entrepreneur of your choice.[15] My wife and I loaned $25 to a woman in Togo in Africa who needed $1,200 to buy a freezer to enable her to add fish to her array of local produce for sale in her small grocery store. In less than 48 hours she was fully funded by us and other donors, and over the next year she paid us all back in full. We then loaned that same $25 to three women in Pakistan for their entrepreneurial projects. They too paid us back in full within a year.

If you prefer to promote the entrepreneurial spirit right here in your own backyard, you will be glad to know that Kiva has now added small-scale American entrepreneurs to its list of potential loan recipients. If you believe in capitalism, put your money where your mouth is. Loan some money to promote the cause around the world or right here at home.

> *Recently, Kiva has revealed that it allocates money before donors select recipients. Since money is fungible, this ultimately makes no difference if all Kiva-approved projects get fully funded. This seems to be the case since the projects offered at Kiva.org attract donors quickly and are generally fully funded in short order.*

Freedom and democracy in China

World history has displayed two different freedoms: external freedom (freedom from foreign domination) and internal freedom (democracy). People tend to sacrifice internal freedom whenever they are subjected to external threats.

Dictators and quasi-dictators from Fidel Castro and Hugo Chavez to Kim Jong Il and Mahmoud Ahmadinejad have thrived on this effect. Even in the United States after 9/11 we allowed more surveillance including government wire-tapping and data collection when we felt threatened. We did this in spite of the fact that since our revolution we have never been subjected to foreign domination.

China has a different history. In the 19th and early 20th centuries, key parts of China were subjugated by a variety of colonial powers. In the late 1930s and early 1940s, China suffered enormously under brutal domination by the Japanese military. Do we really want to be viewed as just another country trying to bully China by telling it what to do? During World War II, Chinese peasants rescued our pilots at the risk of entire Chinese villages being wiped out by the Japanese military in retaliation. We needed each other's friendship then, and we need it now.

China lives in a hostile and unstable region of the world. Recently a North Korean submarine torpedoed a South Korean warship. The South Koreans cut off trade relations with the North. The North Koreans threatened all out war. A while back a Russian warship sank a Chinese cargo ship after a disagreement over a rice shipment. Eight Chinese crewmen were declared missing and presumed dead. China needs our friendship, and we need China's. Let's be China's friend, not her enemy.

China could have taken the money earned by selling us their products at a discount (favorable exchange rate) and used it to build lots of warships and armaments. Instead China reinvested most of that money back into America via its sovereign wealth funds.[16] When Bath Iron Works in Bath, Maine, needed a 750-foot, 28,000-ton dry dock for building our most advanced guided missile destroyers, China's Jiangdu Yuchai Shipbuilding Company built it for us for $27 million.[17]

Some commentators have referred to our interdependent economies as *Chimerica*.[18] We need to continue building a strong partnership with China and not foolishly undermine it.[19]

Internally China went through the trauma of the Cultural Revolution. Chairman Mao incited young people to rise up against all educated people. Many Chinese leaders today have parents, grandparents or other relatives who were abused, tortured or murdered. Some are survivors of imprisonment and abuse themselves. Fear of foreign domination and internal turmoil is not just a concern of the Chinese leadership but also of the Chinese people themselves.

In November 2008 we were again able to completely "overthrow" our own government via the ballot box. We were able to change presidents without spilling even a few crumbs at the pre-inaugural White House coffee. Not every country is so fortunate. Widespread riots and turmoil in China are in no one's interest. The recent rioting and bloodshed in Thailand is just a small example.

China may not be a democracy in the European or American sense, but it is not a brutal dictatorship. No doubt people have been held without a fair trial as we have done at Guantánamo. No doubt some have been abused as we did at Abu Ghraib. The best thing we can do to encourage other countries to respect human rights is to actually respect human rights ourselves.

Ultimately the Chinese people will determine in their own way if and when they are ready for a full democracy of the people, by the people and for the people. If our government tries to force its own views on China, it will only rally the Chinese people around their government and motivate them to sacrifice more internal freedom to maintain their external independence.

Cheap Chinese tires challenge
Obama trade strategy

Since this was written, President Obama has signed an order for a 35 percent tariff on Chinese tires. Obama's gesture is pointless since the tariff is temporary and applies only to China. Low income American consumers should not worry. Wal-Mart will find cheap tires from another low-wage country to quickly fill the gap.

President Obama must make a key decision about which way to lead America in the 21st century. Should he hit consumers with a 55 percent increase in the price of

131

imported Chinese tires at Wal-Mart and other discount tire outlets to protect workers at American tire manufacturing plants and risk retaliatory curbs on American exports? Or, should he resist union demands to fend off the cheap Chinese tires? Cooper Tire in Albany, GA has already laid off over 2,000 workers. The kind of low quality tires in question are not even currently produced in the United States so no jobs are actually at stake.

Under a law passed by Congress in 2000 and agreed to by China when it joined the World Trade Organization, the United States can impose a temporary tariff when a surge in imports from China threatens to hurt a U.S. industry. In July 2009 the U.S. International Trade Commission determined that the U.S. tire industry was so threatened that a 55 percent tariff should be imposed on tires from China. Under the Bush administration such recommendations were often ignored. Obama must decide by a Sept. 17, 2009 deadline or we forgo temporary tariff protection.

Should Obama lead the country bravely toward the new knowledge economy of the 21st century or backward to try to re-establish the physical work economy of the 20th century? Many people believe that we cannot trust the virtual economy of bits and bytes to provide solid jobs for the future. Instead they want us to try to reestablish the economy of physical atoms that was so reassuring in the 20th century. Which path should Obama take in leading the country?

Does our future lie in raising prices in Wal-Mart and other discount stores where most Americans shop or in keeping prices low and leading our country toward the knowledge-based jobs of the 21st century? Some claim that we will never be able to compete with China with its low-wage workers even as shortages of such workers in China began to emerge just prior to the recent recession. China in turn has been losing out to low-wage workers in Vietnam and other Southeast Asian countries. Africans no doubt will eventually take their turn in taking possession of low-wage jobs.

China has already figured this out and is moving to raise the knowledge intensity and quality of its products and the education of its people. President Obama knows this is the future, but his party faces elections in 2010. In the 2008 election he promised to protect American jobs from "unfair" foreign competition.

Foreign competition is only "unfair" in this sense if there are a fixed number of jobs. Economists know this idea as the "lump of labor" fallacy.[20] In reality the number and quality of jobs is very dynamic and determined by the forces of supply and demand. Fiscal and monetary policy contribute to new demand along with rising export demand. New demand is being generated all the time for new products that didn't even exist in the 20th century. The problem is that old workers are trained in old, unskilled jobs or skilled jobs like welding or fork lift operations which are becoming automated as computers take over in manufacturing. Manufacturing production is not declining in America, but rather it is manufacturing employment that is declining in the face of "lights out" manufacturing where robots work through the night with no complaints and few breaks.[21] Many of the jobs going to China would have gone to robots anyway. The jobs going to China, on to Vietnam and then on to Africa are just stopping briefly on their way to oblivion.

If you want job security in the 21st century don't learn welding. Instead learn what a relational database is. Learn a computer programming language. Learn how to use sampling to estimate the probability of an unlikely event. Learn how to create and use a collaborative filter. Learn what a Taylor series expansion is. Learn how to put together a business plan and how to determine if a business process is scalable or not scalable. These basics and many more can be learned on your own through Google search or Bing! Some of what you need to know to compete in the 21st century can be found in Wikipedia.

China's old guard leadership came from the engineering class. They understand all this. They know these low-wage manufacturing jobs are a flash in the pan that won't last. They are preparing China for the 21st century. It is much easier for them. They have no voters hanging on to the past to stand in their way. President Obama knows this, but must deal with the next election.

8. Terrorism & Middle East:
Iran, Israel, profiling, no-fly

The idea that human life is priceless and no sane and sensible person would ever want to die doesn't hold up under close examination. In *The Tale of Two Cities*[1] Charles Dickens tells the story of Sydney Carton, who willingly goes to the guillotine by switching places with Charles Darnay. Then there was that passenger in the plane that crashed in the Potomac a few years back who kept passing the life ring to fellow passengers. His generosity cost him his life as he slipped exhausted below the surface. Terrorists have entirely different reasons, but are just as willing to sacrifice themselves. For better or for worse people want to leave their mark and some are willing to give up their lives to do so.

The first three selections in this chapter suggest that dealing with the terrorist menace in the short run may involve greater scrutiny of each person's body and behavior. In the longer term, however, we must deal with both the Palestinian conflict and the belligerent Iranian theocracy. Scientific studies suggest that democracy is difficult to sustain when education and per capita income levels are low. Several key players such as King Abdullah II of Jordan and Prime Minister Netanyahu of Israel know this. President Obama's move to shift strategic missile defense to focus more squarely on Iran makes sense in the short run, but a longer term strategy to bring peace to the Middle East is needed. The key to solving both the Middle East conflict and terrorism is more education and business development in Palestine and more respect for and solidarity with Iranian protestors.

Can profiling stop terrorists?

Umar Farouk Abdulmutallab, who has been charged with attempting to blow up Northwest Flight 253 from Amsterdam to Detroit on Christmas Day 2009, was not recruited by al-Qaeda in Yemen. He sought them out. Could better profiling at our airports have stopped him or others like him?[2]

What do virtually all terrorists have in common? They are loners who are bitter and alienated from society. They feel under-appreciated or rejected and want revenge. They justify their actions as a political statement rather than settlement of a personal dispute. Abdulmutallab is just the latest in a long list of such individuals. He found acceptance and support for his mission of revenge with radical Islamic extremists at University College London as a student there from 2005 to 2008.

How is Abdulmutallab different from Fort Hood accused murderer Major Nidal Malik Hasan,[3] anti-abortionist killer Scott Roeder[4] or Oklahoma bomber Timothy McVeigh?[5] Each felt the need for an excuse to get their revenge. For Abdulmutallab and Hasan it was a twisted version of radical Islam while Roeder used anti-abortionist rhetoric and McVeigh an anti-government theology to justify acts of depravity. Islamic, pro-life and limited-government concerns were used as smoke screens for bad behavior. They differ in their means. Hasan and Roeder used the relatively low technology of guns while Abdulmutallab and McVeigh exploited knowledge of bomb making.

The problem with profiling is that the real threat comes from angry people who want revenge. Such individuals redefine themselves as martyrs for a cause to gain access to better methods and materials. They will latch on to any cause that seems useful in achieving their deadly aims. The potential supply of such individuals is endless. Consequently, profiling is limited in usefulness especially at airport checkpoints. Virtually anyone can use extreme Hollywood makeup techniques to disguise themselves as a harmless old lady in a flowered dress. The electronic, virtual strip-search, scanning machines may violate privacy, but they may be much more effective at ferreting out disguised terrorists than profiling.

The real bottleneck in the terrorist pipeline is in access to bomb materials that cannot be easily detected. The source of these specialized materials needs to be restricted. Companies manufacturing explosives can be required by law to include a tracing substance that identifies the source of the explosive. Scanning for them at airports is important, but drying up their source would be even better. Profiling is more of a distraction than a solution. The number of nut jobs out there is just too big. It's the concentrated, *undetectable* bomb materials that are in short supply.

Make 90-day no-fly the default for terrorists

Pundits and politicians have been mulling over how much evidence is sufficient to put someone on the no-fly list. Perhaps it would be wiser to "shoot" first and ask questions later.

Now that Umar Farouk Abdulmutallab has appeared in court for allegedly attempting to blow up Northwest Flight 253 from Amsterdam to Detroit on Christmas Day, we have had some time to reflect on what went wrong. Apparently intelligence was shared among the appropriate intelligence agencies. Analysts had even reached the point of deciding to interview Abdulmutallab upon his arrival in Detroit. But it would have been too late. It is time to make a major change in how our intelligence analysts are allowed to operate.

If you are an intelligence analyst, you should not have to check the regulations to see how much evidence is enough to put someone on the no-fly list. At the slightest suspicion, any intelligence analyst should be authorized to immediately place any suspect on the no-fly list for 90 days. During the 90-day period the evidence could be reviewed to determine if the suspect's name should remain on the no-fly list or should be removed.

Ordinarily our system works best by assuming innocence until guilt is proven. In this new world of terrorism and asymmetric warfare we need to make an exception to that rule when many lives are simultaneously at risk. When the lives of airplane passengers are in danger, our intelligence analysts need to be able to reverse the usual presumption and assume a terrorist suspect guilty for a temporary period of 90 days unless cleared. A 90-day period should be sufficient to get other analysts to weigh in and decide whether the danger is great enough to keep the person on the no-fly list or allow the name to automatically revert to its pre-alert status.

In the fast moving world of innovative terrorism, we can't wait until some new, unusual terrorist method is fully understood. As Malcolm Gladwell points out in his book *Blink*,[6] an expert's immediate gut reaction based on a great deal of experience is, more often than not, right on target. Unnecessarily inconveniencing an innocent traveler for 90 days is not too high a price to pay for protecting the lives of a plane full of people.

Psychiatrist Nidal Malik Hasan programmed himself for murder

Nidal Malik Hasan did not hide what he was doing to himself in the time leading up to his deranged attack on his fellow soldiers at Fort Hood in 2009. He was clearly on a one-way track to disaster.

Starting several years before the attack, Hasan told many people about his belief that the Army's mission in the Middle East was in conflict with his Islamic religious convictions. When he and his peers were asked to give presentations on a medical topic of their choice, he gave a presentation on how he thought that his religion conflicted with his Army mission. The inappropriateness of his talk by itself should have alerted his superiors that he was off-track.

He knew as a psychiatrist that he could not maintain a high level of cognitive dissonance for an extended period. The only surprise was that others did not catch on to what he was doing.

To understand what he did, consider how the human mind works. The complexity of our world is beyond the capacity of any human to fully comprehend. Every day we are forced to simplify things to make them manageable. The truth lies in the uniqueness of every person and every situation we encounter. As we simplify things in our minds, we move away from the truth.

Categorizing, labeling and, I dare say, stereotyping people and events are all part of the simplification process. Simplification is unavoidable because without it we would be overwhelmed with detail we could not manage. Hasan's first mistake was in not realizing that simplification does not move one toward the truth but away from it.

It is easier to say that most people in the Middle East are Muslims than to say that while most are Muslims, there are other religions and within the Muslim faith there are many different ethnic identities. After all, our own government initially failed to understand the Sunni versus Shiite conflict in Iraq. Moreover, Hasan ignored the fact that we defended Muslims in Bosnia and Kosovo against Serbs, who are predominately Orthodox Christian.[7] He also ignored the fact that the governments we are supporting in Iraq, Afghanistan and Pakistan are also predominantly Muslim.

The first lesson we should learn from Hasan's horrible behavior is that oversimplification can be dangerous and cause someone to take things too far. Watch out for people who think they've got complex issues boiled down to a few simple slogans. Data reduction is necessary for decision making but should be accompanied by a strong dose of humility.

The second lesson is that it takes a while for someone to program themselves in preparation for the type of violent attack that Hasan carried out. People don't just jump out of bed one morning and say "I guess I'll carry out a terrorist attack today." Hasan had to gradually convince himself of the "righteousness" of what he was going to do. Programming your subconscious mind to commit terror takes time and persistence. Repeating simple ideas and slogans over and over again ultimately changes a person's subconscious thoughts, attitudes and actions.

Whether the Fort Hood tragedy should be classified as a terrorist attack or just the product of a deranged mind is not the point. Labeling it what you want doesn't change the reality of this awful event. Here again is what President Obama might call a "teachable moment." We all need to be more alert to people who are programming themselves for disaster, whether it be in preparation for a terrorist attack or a simple suicide.

Strange strategy backfires: Iranian President Ahmadinejad fools no one except himself

Iranian President Mahmoud Ahmadinejad decided to accept the withdrawal of his choice for vice president, Esfandiar Rahim Mashaie. He gave up on a strategy that fooled no one. He now finds himself and his hard-line buddies more isolated than ever.[8]

Mashaie had said earlier that Iran had no quarrel with the people of Israel but just with their government's policies. Under orders from supreme leader Ayatollah Ali Khamenei and strong objections from hard-liners, Ahmadinejad threw in the towel and gave up his ruse to mollify those seeking a more moderate stand toward Israel.

Did he really think that Israel and its supporters would have been fooled by his choice of vice president? With hard-liners dominating virtually every aspect of Iranian life, the nomination of Mashaie was more of an insulting joke than a real attempt to signal a significant change in policy.

Now that the smoke has cleared, the spotlight can once again reveal a regime so extreme and so desperate that it does not know which way to turn. One can only hope that it will collapse in confusion and disarray before long. It certainly seems to be heading in that direction.

The supporters of opposition presidential candidate Mir Hossein Mousavi should take heart. Ahmadinejad's erratic behavior will only hasten his downfall and that of his ignominious regime.[9]

Obama drops missile shield
to end cold war strategy

The White House dropped its plans to put anti-ballistic missiles in Poland[10] and a missile detection radar station in the Czech Republic.[11] Instead it will strategically place interceptors closer to Iran such as on ships in the Persian Gulf. If this marks the end of the Cold War strategy of isolating Russia, it could have profound effects on both U.S.-Russian relations and Russian politics.

Old generals are always preparing for the last war, in this case the cold-war. More often than not, such thinking distracts from focusing on new threats, in this case Iran. Thinking of Russia as another "evil empire" is at best naive and at worst a recipe for disaster. It has also caused Russia and the United States to follow foolish policies. The timing of this decision could not be better with Prime Minister Putin and President Medvedev just starting to sort out who will be Russia's next president.

The United States has too often reverted to its Cold War strategy of isolating Russia instead of encouraging Russia to work toward joining the World Trade Organization (WTO) and eventually the European Union (EU). Russia, for its part, has followed policies that will undermine its own long-term stability in both politics and economics. Every far-sighted country needs to provide for the peaceful "overthrow" of its own government. It's not just that "power corrupts and absolute power corrupts absolutely" but that a government in power too long runs out of fresh ideas and loses touch with the people.

Suppressing debate and discussion in a free press allows too few people to dominate government policies for far too long. Medvedev's chances of remaining president and taking Russia in a more open, productive and friendly direction will be enhanced by the Obama decision.

Both Russia and the United States have followed foolish energy policies in recent years. The United States assumed that oil and natural gas prices wouldn't rise too much while Russia planned for higher carbon fuel prices. To gain immediate advantage, Putin directed Russia to reverse energy privatization in Russia through direct and indirect means. Government revenues in Russia are largely dependent on oil and gas. What economists call the *Dutch disease*[12] makes a country's non-fuel exports exorbitantly expensive in world markets when its currency's value is driven up by the demand for its oil and gas. This prevents a country from developing and diversifying its economy. Petro-dictatorships develop when a country becomes too dependent on its carbon fuel exports.[13] Putin's strategy is very short-sighted. Hopefully Medvedev will gain the upper hand and take Russia in a wiser direction with a new long-term strategy.

Obama and Medvedev need to work together to help Russia prepare to join the WTO and eventually the EU by diversifying its economy and encouraging independent news media to allow for viable alternative political parties in Russia.[14] Obama's decision to drop the nuclear missile shield could have potentially far-reaching consequences. We can only hope that it will truly *reset* Russian-American relations and be just the beginning of changes in key Russian and American policies.

Netanyahu reverses peace prosperity logic

For years Israeli leaders have urged Palestinian leaders to make peace with Israel as a path to prosperity for the Palestinian people. In an interview[15] with Charlie Rose on PBS taped prior to his speech to the United Nations, Israeli Prime Minister Benjamin Netanyahu reversed this logic. In his interview, the prime minister recognized the importance of improving the economic condition of the Palestinian people as part of the path to peace. While he didn't offer direct assistance, he did emphasize that Israel will do what it can to enhance the economy of the West Bank.

Social scientists have studied the prosperity-democracy-peace nexus for many years. With exceptions such as India notwithstanding, a stable, long-lasting democracy generally requires approximately $6,000 of income per person.[16] Democracy is quite fragile in countries with lower per capita incomes (e.g. Honduras: $3,100).

2008 CIA World Factbook	
Israel	$26,800
Iran	$8,700
Lebanon	$5,700
Jordan	$5,100
Egypt	$4,200
Syria	$4,100
Iraq	$2,900
Afghanistan	$800

Figure 4. Per capita income

Figure 4 shows the average income per person as GDP per capita. Countries with low average incomes along with low levels of education are not good candidates for democracy.

(8.) TERRORISM & MIDDLE EAST

King Abdullah of Jordan raised this issue with President Bush concerning the Iraq invasion noting that Iraq's per capita income is less than half the required amount. Obviously President Bush was not persuaded.[17]

The bottom line is that a life of poverty is a life without hope. People with something to live for do not become suicide bombers. It is not enough to offer a vague promise of prosperity after peace. Instead Prime Minister Netanyahu now recognizes the importance of improved economic conditions as an important aspect of the path toward peace.

The formula is simple and has been repeated again and again throughout modern history. Rising per capita income (and education) promotes stable democracy, and stable democracies do not attack one another.

One caveat to the income-democracy hypothesis is that countries where the government is highly dependent on oil and natural gas resources can fail to maintain stable democracy even with higher per capita incomes. Venezuela with a per capita income of $7,200 and Russia with $12,200 raise this concern. Petro-dictatorships form when the people become too dependent on government handouts and foreign demand for oil and natural gas drives the value of a country's currency so high that its other products are priced out of world markets. Recent Iranian demonstrators have been very much aware of this pernicious effect of their country's dependency on oil and natural gas revenues.[18]

For peace in the Middle East and democracy to thrive, regional incomes must rise and governments dependent on natural resources for the bulk of their revenues must diversify. King Abdullah II of Jordan has understood this for some time. Now Israeli Prime Minister Netanyahu is getting the idea.

9. Afghanistan:
elections, stability, U.S. troops

The outcome of the conflict in Afghanistan will depend on the interaction between Afghan politics and American politics. Without real election reform in Afghanistan it will be hard to sustain American support for our involvement in Afghanistan.

At the same time we see the interaction between Taliban forces and American forces, with the Afghan people in the middle. Winning the hearts and minds of the people of America and Afghanistan will also depend to a great extent on how our military treats the Afghan people, especially in comparison to their treatment by the Taliban.

To understand whether an early American withdrawal from Afghanistan will end our terrorism problem, we need to look to the Russian experience in Chechnya rather than our own experience in Vietnam. The second essay discusses how Russia's Chechnya experience in some ways mirrors the possible outcome we face in Afghanistan.

The third essay is about how our military is analyzing the complex, dynamic relationships that will determine the success or failure of our policies, strategies and tactics in Afghanistan. It is impossible to adequately analyze such problems in our heads. Fortunately we have computers to assist us in sorting out the factors that influence important outcomes such as our success or failure in Afghanistan. The United States Army at Fort Leavenworth teaches our military leadership about complex, dynamic systems. However, I discovered on a recent visit there that while our military leaders were being introduced to such ideas conceptually, most of them were not given any actual experience in formulating such a system and running it on a computer to simulate possible outcomes. Until our military leaders get hands-on experience with system dynamic simulations, all that talk will not be enough to allow them to effectively use this very important analytical tool.

The fourth essay sees some hope for Afghanistan as the Afghani parliament blocks many of President Karzai's cabinet appointments. Sorting out corrupt from qualified nominees is not an easy task, but it appears that the Afghani parliament is on the right track in represent-ing the best interests of the people of Afghanistan.

The last essay looks at the future of the "Human Terrain System" strategy that has been under way for several years but has just recently become more widely deployed. In the past the emphasis for soldiers has been how to increase their firepower. Their rifles serve to enhance their physical strength. In the future the emphasis will be on enhancing a soldier's mental powers. The "Human Terrain System" strategy is a first step in that direction.

Afghan election fraud hard pill to swallow

It's difficult to ask Americans to send their courageous soldiers to fight and possibly die in Afghanistan for a corrupt, fraudulent kleptocracy.

If there was ever a case for declaring an election fraudulent, this is it. It is not sufficient for President Hamid Karzai to admit that some of his supporters showed some bias in his favor. From all reports, the level of fraud in the Afghan election was quite extensive to say the least. Reports included such things as more votes than voters and Karzai getting all the votes in some districts of an opponent's home region.[1]

It's bad enough to have to write off a great deal of corruption and influence peddling as just a bit of traditional Afghan tribal politics. Wholesale vote rigging is another story. No amount of cultural excuses will soften this hard reality.

The Vietnam conflict demonstrated that wars can be lost just as easily in America as on the foreign battlefield. Both President Karzai and President Obama must now face the fact that winning in Afghanistan, however that may be defined, requires winning the hearts and minds of Americans just as surely as it requires winning the hearts of minds of Afghanis.

Obama and Karzai must acknowledge that elections in Afghanistan must be reasonably free and fair if they want the American people to continue to send their loyal sons and daughters to fight in this war.

Afghanistan mirrors Chechnya, not Vietnam

The challenge the United States faces in Afghanistan is more analogous to what Russia faced in Chechnya than our own experience in Vietnam. Understanding what happened in Chechnya may help us avoid similar pitfalls in Afghanistan. Even withdrawal from Chechnya did not end attacks in Russia by Chechen extremists.

The First Chechen War lasted from 1994 to 1996. It was much shorter than our involvement in Vietnam, but ended with Russian troops leaving after being unsuccessful in attempting to subdue the insurrection in

Chechnya. The insurgents had the advantage of very mountainous terrain and eventually attacked the capital, Grozny. The battle for Grozny produced a bloodbath that convinced the Russian public that enough was enough. The Russians then agreed to a ceasefire and a year later signed a peace treaty. Up to that point the technical aspects at least were like a mini-version of our experience in Vietnam.[2]

The new president of Chechnya did not completely control the various ethnic tribes but eventually declared Sharia law in Chechnya. In spite of the peace treaty, insurgents from Chechnya attacked neighboring Dagestan with the declared intent of establishing a union of Chechnya and Dagestan. Dagestan is another republic in the Russian Federation right next to Chechnya (think Pakistan) with shared ethnic ties to Chechnya (think Pashtun).

What happened next might be called Russia's 9/11 experience. A series of similar bombings that took place in Russia were blamed on the Chechen separatists. A bomb went off at a shopping center in Moscow in August 1999 followed within weeks by numerous bombings at apartment buildings and elsewhere in Moscow and several other Russian cities that killed hundreds of Russians. A previously unknown group called the *Liberation Army of Dagestan* claimed responsibility.[3]

This is somewhat different from our experience in Vietnam, but somewhat similar to what has happened and is happening in Afghanistan. Unlike Vietnam, there are no nations openly supporting the enemy forces in Chechnya and Afghanistan, although there are approximately 4,000 foreigners fighting alongside the Taliban in Afghanistan, including many from Chechnya. Although US allies have come mostly from NATO countries, Russia,

India and China have a more immediate interest in our success in Afghanistan, not to mention Pakistan and, with some mixed feelings, Iran.

However, the similarity to Vietnam may yet emerge. If President Obama allows us to get bogged down in a protracted war in Afghanistan he may eventually split the Democratic Party, and we may see Vietnam-style demonstrations once again on the streets in America.

How to determine if we can achieve stability in Iraq and Afghanistan

Everyone knows the curious fact that when you square a number between zero and one, it gets smaller, but if you square a number greater than one, it gets bigger. What many don't know is that these facts are important for determining if our policies in Iraq and Afghanistan will ultimately lead to stability.

In a recent visit to the School of Advanced Military Studies (SAMS) at Fort Leavenworth,[4] I came to realize that the SAMS program was essentially an MBA program on how to design a paradigm to explain how our military can be successful in the post Cold War era. I came away impressed with their MBA program, but also believing that what SAMS really needs is an expanded Ph.D. program.

A favorite theme in the SAMS program is the study of complexity in dynamic systems.[5] Both Iraq and Afghanistan represent dynamic systems. Giving people jobs represents a *positive* feedback loop: Jobs give people money, which allows them to buy things, spurring demand and production, and leading to more job growth. Al-Qaeda[6] extremists who get carried away with their fanaticism represent a *negative* feedback loop: The more extreme they get, the more the people rise up to resist them. A dynamic system contains many positive and negative feedback loops.[7] Outcome variables might include unemployment rate, electricity and water availability, extent of fair and free voting, bombings and violent deaths.

The stability of a dynamic system can be determined by numbers called "eigenvalues." If the standardized eigenvalues of the system lie between minus one and plus one, then the system is stable because squaring them drives them towards zero. However, if any of the eigenvalues lie "outside of the unit circle" (which is centered at zero), then the system is inherently unstable.[8] A stable system will converge to an equilibrium, hopefully a good equilibrium. The Army needs to develop system dynamic models in order to run simulations to see if proposed policies and strategies lead to a stable, desirable equilibrium.

In the SAMS program it is fun to talk about complexity and the stability of dynamic systems. In particular people like to talk about how chaos theory tells us that a butterfly flapping its wings in Brazil can cause hurricanes in Florida. However, for a system to be chaotic, its "Lyapunov exponent" must be greater than one. Chaos and catastrophes in dynamic systems are not abstract concepts, they are precise mathematical conditions.[9] Just throwing those terms around without doing the math is like a young child who likes to talk vaguely about the sex act but doesn't know precisely what it is or how to do it.

As a dynamic system goes through time its eigenvalues get squared at every iteration.* Repeatedly

---

* *This is a special case used here for expository purposes. The exponent is not limited to integers or even rational numbers. The*

152

squaring an eigenvalue outside of the unit circle causes it to get bigger and bigger so that over time the system explodes into chaos. You don't know if the system is inherently unstable unless you calculate the eigenvalues.[10] You have to *do the math*. My fear is that in the SAMS program, not everyone knows how to do the math or even why it is important to do the math.

Our soldiers have shown great courage in facing enemy fire. They will need a different kind of courage to face the equations. We can only hope that the SAMS program will lead the way in getting student soldiers to *do the math*.

Obama's Afghan "Human Terrain" strategy

Past wars have focused on capturing key territory or killing as many of the enemy as possible. These objectives do not hold sway in Afghanistan. President Obama's new "Human Terrain System" strategy[11] is more like his 2008 election campaign than any war we've ever experienced. Will it work?

Not since President Kennedy appointed Robert McNamara as his Secretary of Defense have so many "whiz kid" intellectuals been involved with the planning and execution of military strategy.

Following up on the strategy General David Petraeus began in Iraq, social scientists under the leadership of Montgomery McFate are retraining our soldiers to learn the social structure of Afghan villages, towns and provinces. They hold meetings with tribal elders, take notes and record the GPS coordinates of every

actual power may depend upon the structure of the particular dynamic system including its data and restrictions imposed upon it.

encounter. The objective is not so much to kill our enemies as to convert them.

David Axe's report *Social Scientists Under Fire* provides a detailed in-country account of how this new strategy works in the latest issue of *Miller-McCune*. Also, see reports and analysis directly from Afghanistan of Kansas City Star Midwest Voices columnist Major Grant Martin at http://voices.kansascity.com/

Has our military leadership gone soft in the head, or are they just now beginning to use their heads to solve the problem we should have solved in Vietnam?

The body count measure of success assumes a fixed number of enemy combatants. What if the number of enemy is dynamically changing day by day and hour by hour? They don't wear uniforms, and they easily blend back into the population. We can kill a small number and a few innocent civilians, or a large number and a lot of civilians.[12]

Can we convert them faster than we can kill them? Convincing the Taliban to work within a democratic framework and to help us track down al-Qaeda may be a more reasonable strategy. After all, why would Afghan villagers want foreigners from Pakistan and elsewhere to control their lives? We can help them get rid of all those pushy foreigners.

The key is to show more respect for the villagers and know more about the villagers than the Taliban do. Right now our soldiers are jotting down notes and GPS coordinates. They have a satellite link, but need more. Our MQ-1 Predator drones accompany each mission overhead to provide air support in case of a Taliban assault or significant attack. Why not use our drones as mobile cell phone towers? We already control our drones in second-by-second operations from thousands of miles away in Nellis Air Force Base in Nevada. Would it be that hard to link up our troops a few thousand feet below to our drones and then on to Bagram Airbase near Kabul?

Wouldn't it be useful to have a "reference librarian" communicating live from a computer at Bagram Airbase reviewing everything known about that village and its citizens. "Ask Aaraam about his cousin Asif who recently broke his leg," our librarian could suggest. At first Afghans would be startled by our knowledge of their village, but then they would get used to it. Before long they would see us as their friends.

The "Human Terrain System" strategy of changing from killing to converting means switching the focus from the latest variant of the M-16 rifle to a new kind of helmet for our soldiers. You could call the new helmet an iPhone-in-a-hat. Each soldier's helmet would become a small computer with a tiny camera on the front, a microphone, a speaker and voice recognition software. Just as the rifle enhances the muscle power, the helmet can enhance the brain power.

Each soldier's helmet could be trained to recognize that soldier's voice. With voice recognition and instant computer translation, the soldier's helmet speaker could translate perfectly into Pashto, Dari or whatever language is spoken in that village.

Since the translation software could not be calibrated quickly enough to translate a villager's voice, and we cannot assign a translator in the field to each of our soldiers, a translator in Bagram could hear the villager speaking and translate in real time via the drone cell phone link. Simultaneous translation goes on every day in the General Assembly of the United Nations in New York. Why not provide our soldiers with the benefits of simultaneous translation out there in the field in Afghanistan?

Concentrating our translators at Bagram allows them to switch between our soldiers in the field at the moment each soldier encounters a villager. Our best translators would be busy translating all the time instead of tromping through the fields wasting valuable translation time.

All conversations and pictures would be recorded for analysis and data mining. Our national security analysts are already skilled at this job.

In Vietnam we talked about winning the hearts and minds of the people, but were unable to do it. McNamara and his whiz kids failed. Maybe this time it will work.

10. Attitudes and Beliefs:
underlying, behavioral motivation and incentives

S ometimes we deceive ourselves with mental models of the world around us that mislead us. Since we have limited mental energy, we use expectations that fit our mental models to fix our beliefs so we don't have to expend brain power rethinking something all over again every time we encounter it.

Racial beliefs and attitudes are a case in point. People held inaccurate racial mental models for many years and are only now gradually realizing that the old axion "You can't tell a book by its cover" applies to people as well. The first selection discusses the evolution of racial attitudes in America since World War II. The interaction of racial attitudes with attitudes toward police, as well as police attitudes toward people, is addressed in the second selection.

The third and fourth selections in this chapter are both about how we operate our motor vehicles. Here too our beliefs are captured in mental models and expectations about how the world works. Too many people think that texting-while-driving isn't all that dangerous, but recent studies reveal exactly the opposite. People also have a general sense of how much risk they are comfortable with. Requiring seat belts and motorcycle helmets makes people feel safer. Economists have discovered that requiring the use of safety equipment frees people up to engage in riskier behavior so they can return to their equilibrium level of risk tolerance.

Research studies have shown that requiring seat belt use reduces injuries and deaths but increases risky driving which, in turn, generates more accidents. By gaining a better understanding of people's mental models, we can better predict how proposed policies will affect their behavior.

The last two selections address the mental models that some people use in their consumption behavior. If your mental model of the world makes you feel guilty for having more than others, you will be glad to see others rise to attain your level of well-being. On the other hand, if you can feel good about yourself only when you are doing better than others, you will be continually trying to outdo them.

The last selection is closely related in that it notes that some people value things according to their price. If your mental model sees price as indicative of value, you can outdo others by acquiring pricier possessions. Some mental models lead us toward equality and contentment, while others take us toward inequality and avarice.

Darwin, race and racial attitudes in America

The 200th anniversary of Darwin's birth is an appropriate time to reflect on what Darwin's evolutionary theories imply about race.[1]

As a white child in the late 1940s and early 1950s, I was bombarded by racial stereotypes. Initially played by two black-faced white guys, the radio and TV show *Amos 'n' Andy* pretended to portray two bumbling African-American businessmen.[2] Discrimination was everywhere. Many people back then thought that blacks were inferior. Extremists tried to justify this using Darwin's theories to claim that blacks were separate on the evolutionary tree. It's hard to imagine now, but segregation was strictly enforced with schools that were separate and unequal.

However, my own experience as a child told me that blacks were much smarter than they were depicted in the media. My father grew up in a household with black servants. I sensed his deep respect for them. Each morning my mother would take me along as she drove my father to the commuter train station. Along the way, my father would wave to a black man at a bus stop. I asked my father who the man was. My father said: "I don't actually know him, but we wave to one another each day."

After my grandparents died, my father took me along to their home where he had arranged to meet with one of their black servants. He wanted the man's advice on how best to prepare the home for sale. The man saw my discolored and infected thumb and told my father that he should take me to the hospital emergency room immediately. The doctors said that advice saved my thumb as gangrene was about to set in. The media depicted blacks as dumb, but my own experience told me they were smart. I could also see how unfair all this was.

In 1963 at the start of my first year in college I joined the NAACP. I marched in plenty of northern protests, but I failed to go down to the South to protest. Instead I helped out at a school on Saturdays that tutored young African-American preschoolers.[3]

Physical differences between blacks and whites are fundamentally due to where their ancestors lived in recent centuries. In recent years I got interested in racial differences in prostate cancer. I noticed patterns in seemingly unrelated medical studies. For example, African Americans are more prone to prostate cancer than whites.[4] In the United States prostate cancer is generally more prevalent in northern states than in southern states. The prostate needs adequate amounts of vitamin D to function properly and avoid cancer. About 90 percent of our vitamin D is generated by sunlight on our skin, and fatty fish have loads of vitamin D.[5] Most people whose ancestors came from northern climates with low intensity sunlight have lighter skin. Eskimos who eat fatty fish with lots of vitamin D have tan skin and lower rates of prostate cancer.[6] Over time, skin color adjusts to climate.

White women living along the equator are prone to loss of folate as the sun leaches folic acid from their bodies. With less folate, white women are prone to miscarriages and having children with birth defects. As our ancestors moved from region to region, dark skin worked better near the equator and white skin fared better farther from the equator.

You don't have to be a rocket scientist or a student of Darwin to get the point. Whites almost surely have black ancestors and blacks almost surely have white ancestors.[7]

A recent report by National Public Radio said that Professor Nina Jablonski, who chairs the Pennsylvania State University Department of Anthropology, has concluded from DNA studies that dramatic changes in skin color have taken place within as few as 100 generations even in the absence of interracial marriage.[8] Professor Jablonski noted that as many families evolved "almost all of us were in a different place and we had a different color."[9]

I have come to appreciate that old protest statement from the 1960s: "We are the ones our parents warned us about." We were closer to the truth even then than we realized. I now understand that we are them, and they are us.

Martin Luther King, Jr. saved America

Some people think that Martin Luther King day is just for African Americans. They could not be more wrong! Dr. King saved us all from what could have been one of America's most horrific tragedies.

We tend to think of the history that happened and ignore the history that didn't happen. But it is the history that didn't happen that makes Martin Luther King, Jr. one of the greatest Americans of all.

Without Martin Luther King, the 1960s could have been a repeat of the bloodshed of the 1860s. The 300 riots that burned down hundreds of stores and homes in cities around America between 1964 and 1968 were just a small taste of what could have happened if Dr. King had not firmly established the nonviolent movement.

What if violent extremists had taken over the Black Liberation movement? We have recently seen how easily even people with good educations and wealthy families can turn into terrorists. People in less fortunate circumstances would have even less to lose.

It's difficult enough to keep foreign suicide bombers out of the United States. What would we do if there were hundreds or even thousands of homegrown suicide bombers ready to give their lives for their cause?

Certainly George Washington and Abraham Lincoln were truly great Americans. Each carried out their duties in extremely difficult times and accomplished great things. But Martin Luther King had to act outside of established power structures. He knew that he would be killed if he kept pushing for justice. He did not have police protection or much protection at all most of the time. He could have stopped at any time and avoided assassination.

Martin Luther King, Jr. was just the right leader at just the right time to save America from itself. African Americans are right to honor Dr. King, but non-African Americans should be equally grateful to the man who saved America.

Sergeant Crowley versus Harvard's Professor Gates

On July 16, 2009 police responded to a 911 call about someone seen breaking into a home in Cambridge, MA. Sgt. James Crowley arrested Harvard professor Henry Louis Gates, Jr., at the residence, which was the professor's home. Some saw this as just another example of racial profiling by police.

Any experienced police reporter for a large city newspaper can provide at least a few names of "rogue" police officers they know. Most police officers are highly trained professionals, but there are almost always a few who think like President Nixon[10] when he said: "When the president does it that means that it is not illegal."

When we were in South Bend, Indiana, my wife and I saw two police officers pull into a Wendy's in their police cruiser. They drove in the exit in defiance of the out-arrow and parked their car across three spaces. When they finished their meal they drove out the entrance against the in-arrow. They were clearly intentionally making an important point: The rules didn't apply to them. They were above the law.

No doubt Sgt. James Crowley felt disrespected by Harvard professor Henry Louis Gates Jr. in their confrontation at Professor Gates' home.[11] There is no doubt that discrimination and racial profiling still exist in some places to some extent. There is also no doubt that

162

some citizens will use anything to get out of being held responsible for their actions, including invoking either their "elite" status if they are well-known or their minority or even handicapped status if that applies.

A police officer can order you to do something if it is legal. A police officer does not have the right to order you to do something that is illegal. Insulting a police officer is not illegal. Here's where it gets complicated. Since you have to follow a police officer's orders as long as they are legal orders, can a police officer legally order you to stop insulting him?

Knowing exacting what was said would help. Digital voice recorders have become very inexpensive. To protect their reputations and that of their departments, in the future all police officers should be required to record all their conversations while on duty. This will both protect them from unfair accusations and protect citizens from unfair treatment.

Should it be illegal to insult important government officials? There are countries where it is illegal to insult the president. If there was such a law in the United States, our jails would be full and a lot of talk radio hosts would be out of business. Realistically, if our presidents are not the recipients of at least some political insults from some of the people, they probably aren't doing their jobs. A good, balanced newspaper knows that it is doing its job well when it gets about half of its insults from liberals and the other half from conservatives.

The problem is that neither police officers nor the general public have a clear idea of where the limits are or should be. We clearly need much more discussion and debate about this issue. In the meantime both citizens and police need to err on the side of caution and not insult or bully one another. If you are a police officer and a citizen insults you, try to ignore it. If you are a citizen who feels that a police officer is acting like a bully, just let it go. You can always file an official complaint later. Patience is a virtue. When it comes to police-citizen relations, it is a very big virtue.

Driving-while-texting (DWT) more dangerous than driving-under-the-influence (DUI)

An Automobile Association of America study shows that driving-while-texting increases the chance of an automobile accident by 50 percent.[12] Another study shows that driving-while-texting (DWT) is considerably more dangerous than driving-under-the-influence (DUI).

One study used simulated driving with a light turning red on the dashboard to represent the car in front stopping suddenly. The study showed that it took longer and a much greater distance for a DWT driver to stop than a DUI driver. According to that study, texting is significantly worse than being drunk behind the wheel.

Mobile phone application company Vlingo reported that 26 percent of mobile phone users admitted to DWT in a recent survey. The survey results ranged from a high of 42 percent in Tennessee to a low of 19 percent in Arizona.

More and more cases are emerging of people losing their son or daughter in a driving-while-texting accident. At the University of Utah, researchers have developed a device they call Key2SafeDriving. It jams all cell phones in a car that has its ignition turned on. The jamming program allows 911 and other special numbers to override the jamming.*

---

* http://www.key2safedriving.net

This problem is not restricted to our highways. Recently a Southern California commuter train engineer ran a red light while texting and caused a train crash that killed 25 people and injured at least 130 others.

We need to pass more state laws that forbid DWT just as we have done with DUI. In 2008 California passed a law to ban holding cell phones while driving. In May 2009 the state police in California issued 12,596 tickets for violations of that law.[13]

What can you do to protect yourself and others from a DWT driver? For starters you can pull over and then call the police on your cell phone to complain. DWT is already illegal in some places.

Second, you can try to stay off highways because traveling straight roads at constant speed tends to facilitate texting. Instead use local roads. Better to get there late and alive on a slower twisting road with lots of stop signs and stop lights that may inhibit texting.

When traffic stops suddenly on a major highway, I used to think that turning on my flashers was enough to warn the cars behind me. Now with all these DWT drivers on the road, I may have to use the horn as well if the cars behind me don't seem to be getting the message.

Seat belt choice: protect people or your car?

Missouri Department of Transportation Director Pete Rahn annoyed state legislators by sending state employees to lobby them for an enhanced seat belt safety law. Consider one key trade-off involved in this issue. Economic research has revealed that while seat belts save lives, they also cause more accidents. Typically people have a level of risk they feel comfortable with and adjust their behavior to take that into account. People who don't wear seat belts are probably more risk prone than those who do. That said, they may be even more dangerous on the road if they are forced to wear seat belts.[14]

Seat belts clearly save lives. They also appear to increase the chances that those who would wear them anyway get involved in an accident caused by someone else.[15] I suppose that if I were a very self-centered person I would want a law passed forbidding anyone from wearing a seat belt except me. Alternatively, we could just pass a law restraining car and truck manufacturers from installing seat belts for drivers.

Without seat belts we would all drive more slowly. After all, force is mass times speed-squared. Just multiply your car's weight times the square of the speed you are traveling. Retired people like me, who don't need to go fast, can afford the time to skip the highways and, instead, take the slower side roads.

When it comes to seat belt legislation, it's your call. The trade-off is clear. Do you want more body bags or more cars in the fix-it shop?

Some Wall Street greed can never be satisfied

Most Wall Street workers are not greedy. My father worked as a stock analyst there for over 30 years. We had a nice home (modest by today's standards) in Westfield, N.J., but just one car. He didn't deceive anyone and his pay was tied to the stock picks he recommended to the board whether they followed his advice or not. His pay directly reflected the accuracy of his predictions. My cousin and uncle worked on Wall Street as well. They were honest, hard-working people.

The problem occurs when there is either deception or inappropriate pay packages that reward failure.

Those who simply seek basic *material wealth* will eventually reach a point of satiation. However, what some may be after is what economists call *positional wealth* which one can obtain only at the expense of another.[16] When a person is in dire poverty, they must focus on their own immediate survival and that of their family. Getting food and shelter is all they want. They are not trying to be better than others. They just want to survive. As people obtain more and more material wealth, some put too much stock in comparing what they've got with others. The "pecking order" is more important to them. They are more interested in acquiring positional wealth.

Most of the stuff that people purchase are what economists call *private goods*, which by definition means that our consumption of each unit of the good denies others the use of that unit. When I eat an apple, it is no longer available for you to eat. In contrast to private goods, there are *public goods* which are defined as goods such that my consumption of a unit of that good does not reduce your ability to consume that same unit.[17] A television show is a good example. My watching a tv show doesn't reduce the availability of that tv show for you to watch. We consume the same show at the same time. In spite of the word "public" most public goods are provided by the private sector.

Positional wealth is based not just on acquiring private goods but rather on acquiring what might be called *super-private goods*. We can define a super-private good as a private good that has the added distinction that the consumption of a unit of the good by one person reduces the pleasure another person gets from consuming another unit of that same good. A huge mansion in a very exclusive location and an exceptionally large, fancy diamond are two examples of super-private goods. The more people have similar goods the less I value mine.

Fortunately, wealth in this world has been shifting from primarily private goods to more and more public goods. As the Internet and related digital products and services account for a larger share of our economy, production involves higher fixed costs such as product development and computer programming and lower variable costs, especially for products available as Internet services or digital downloads. Getting a free music download involves almost zero variable cost. With unlimited digital copies of that music available, my consumption of a unit doesn't reduce the units available to you. Such products are by definition public goods.

But wait, it gets better. Some public goods become more valuable the more others use them. For example, when more of your friends and colleagues are on Facebook, Facebook becomes more valuable to you. Their consumption of the good not only does not diminish your consumption, but instead enhances your consumption of the good. Such a good might be called a *super-public good.* We all benefit as more and more public goods and super-public goods become available.

Greed is not all bad if it motivates hard work. It may be a price we have to pay. But that still leaves us with that unproductive struggle over proportionately fewer and fewer super-private goods. Let the greedy and super greedy duke it out. As they fight more and more over less and less, they may ultimately discover the loneliness that greed brings as they find themselves lost in their enormous mega-mansions wearing their exclusive "priceless" gems. As for the rest of us, let's just concentrate on helping and encouraging one another.

(10.) ATTITUDES AND BELIEFS

What do trademarks and brand names protect?

We all understand the purpose of copyrights and patents. They exist for a limited number of years to allow an individual or company to recoup their high fixed-cost investment. But trademarks[18] and brand names are an entirely different kettle of fish. Why do we have them?

If you are a stylish person, you may be committed to wearing only the most elegant and expensive brand name clothing. You wouldn't be caught dead in an off brand or second-best brand. But when everything else is equal, what makes the best brand best? The price of course!

This reminds me of the Russian joke about two rich Russian oligarchs bragging to one another at an exclusive reception at the Kremlin. The first brags that he paid 10,000 rubles for his tie at Petrovsky's Exquisite Men's Store. The other then replies: "You fool. You paid only 10,000 rubles. You could have purchased exactly the same tie at Dimitri's Fabulous Fashion Wear for 15,000 rubles."

A firm facing serious competition is under pressure to either lower their price or produce a better product. Either way consumers benefit. Consumers do not benefit when competitors engage in price fixing or deceive consumers into thinking that two products are different when they are really identical.

Truth in labeling can play an important role when labeling reflects a real difference in quality or content. Knowing that your computer operating system was made by Apple instead of Microsoft is important. What about otherwise identical products whose brand names only provide a profitable opportunity to exploit blatant elitism?

Lying is still lying so some adverse reaction to misleading labeling is appropriate, but should we spend a lot of taxpayer dollars on enforcement in cases where there is no real difference in quality? Probably not.

Taxpayer money would be better spent enforcing copyrights and patents rather than trademarks** for brand names when differences are in name only. Fines should reflect real differences, not imaginary ones.

** The Lanham Act of 1946 established current trademark law as carried out by the Trademark Trial and Appeals Board.

11. Health Policy:
health insurance, incentives, fat-taxes, doctors and dentists

Providing the best quality medical care at the lowest possible price requires treating each person as the unique individual he or she is and instituting the right incentive structure to guarantee maximum quality care per dollar of health care expenditure.

The first selection in this chapter points out that most medical studies offer predictions for cancer, heart attack or stroke probabilities based on the average values of the variables used in the study. In considering the effect on a particular variable such as cholesterol level on the outcome probability, all other variables are typically held constant at their average values rather than inserting the specific values for a specific patient. This means that the medical advice you get may take into account your particular cholesterol level but uses "Joe Average's" levels for all the other variables. Taking the time to go back to the equations and plug in each patient's specific numbers might significantly improve medical care, considering the nonlinear nature of those equations.

The second selection again emphasizes the importance of incentives in getting the best possible policy outcomes. The medical profession is particularly prone to the use of perverse incentives that produce poor quality results at the highest possible price. Correcting the incentive structure is essential to improving quality care and bringing down costs.[1]

Both fairness and economic efficiency require that we pay for what we get. If I deliberately increase health costs, I should pay for those costs. The third selection examines the moral hazard problem in health insurance where some people deliberately take risks with their health because they know that everyone else will help pay for their foolishness. The most direct way to deal with this problem is to tax the risky products such as cigarettes and unhealthful foods. Pooling risk with insurance works well when we all are equally responsible, but breaks down when some abuse the system.

The fourth selection provides the mathematics that explains why some young libertarians don't buy health insurance. They avoid paying health care premiums but at great risk. They seem determined to follow the "give me liberty or give me death" philosophy.

The fifth selection discusses the term "socialism" which is used as a sort of threat in the health care debate. Upon careful reflection it is easy to see that our society already maintains a balance between socialist and purely private enterprises. It is unlikely that adjusting our position along the spectrum that runs from purely private to totally socialist will create any great upheaval.

The sixth selection again expresses concerns about the lack of attention paid to incentive structures in our health care debate. Without substantial changes in that incentive structure, we cannot expect any significant improvement in health care quality or any significant reduction in health care expenses.

The final selection considers the asymmetric information problem in dental care and the dental fraud that emanates as a result. It offers a modest policy recommendation for making it easier to get a second opinion before proceeding with expensive dental work.

Medical research fails to deliver personal prognosis

What would you think of a financial adviser who ran simulations for you using the average investor's numbers instead of your own? Worse, what if your tax preparer just filled in your tax forms with the average taxpayer's information instead of your specifics?

By analogy, that's what the medical profession is doing. Your doctor wants to treat you as an individual, but in practice it often isn't working out that way. There is a way to substantially improve medical care while significantly reducing costs. The key is how the information from medical studies is actually used in practice.

Your doctor begins by recording your personal and family medical history and orders all sorts of tests and scans. She intends to treat you as a unique individual. But when she turns to the medical literature, it's strictly one size fits all. Physicians interact routinely with drug company representatives, attend conferences and seminars, and have periodic update sessions with medical researchers. The problem is that physicians are told things such as a 1 percent reduction in cholesterol will lead on average to a 2 percent reduction in the probability of a heart attack. But who is this Joe or Jill Average they are talking about? The equations that come from medical research typically use averages from a sample of people. In calculating your probability of dying from a disease, plugging in Joe Average's numbers instead of your own limits its relevance to you.

Research scientists can't calculate the equation that relates cholesterol levels to heart attacks by using your own data alone. To estimate that equation they have to use data from a large number of people. This is necessary for estimation, but not for prediction. To get FDA approval researchers only need to get good results in estimation. Predicting the effect of a drug or procedure on an individual patient is the doctor's job, not the researcher's. Once the equation has been estimated, doctors should use your numbers for the set of explanatory variables in the equation in predicting your probability of having a heart attack. They almost never do this. Instead they use the average numbers from the research study for most of the variables.[2]

For example, the impact of cholesterol on the probability of a heart attack might depend on the iron level in the blood. Iron oxygenizes cholesterol, making it stickier and easier to cling to the walls of your arteries.[3] A pre-menopausal woman tends to have less iron in her blood so the same level of cholesterol is less dangerous for her than for a post-menopausal woman or a man. Researchers typically substitute the average iron level over all patients in their studies for research journals or sponsors. They do this with all the variables, except for cholesterol. In other words, they simulate a one percent reduction in cholesterol using Joe Average's numbers for all the other variables. It would be a lot more accurate to plug in a specific patient's numbers for iron and all the other variables in the model, but researchers know that the doctors are short of time and don't have access to medical software that could personalize the analysis.

Maybe you're a heart attack waiting to happen, or maybe your chances of a heart attack are quite small. You won't know unless they plug in your numbers. President Barack Obama already got a provision in the stimulus bill to provide funding to digitize patient data.[4] This will make your data much easier to analyze. A medical software company could get information from the authors of medical studies that would enable it to more accurately assist doctors in a diagnosis, including red-flagging patients at high risk for a particular illness.[5]

You need to ask your doctor to have your data analyzed. We all need to do this. Doctors should take the initiative and ask for this service. Then they will have time to study the results and incorporate their own first-hand knowledge and experience before choosing specific treatment plans. Until we start asking for this service, it will not become available.

The incentive structure of our health care system is all wrong

To understand any economic system you have to understand the incentive structure. If you examine the incentives in our health care system, you can see why health care costs are out of control. Current incentives for politicians, doctors and patients maximize wasteful, unnecessary health care spending.

(1) A politician cannot run an election campaign without money. Consequently, politicians have designed our health care system to satisfy the medical lobbyists and maximize campaign contributions from the medical establishment, who want to sell more tests, procedures and pills.

(2) Doctors really want to do what is best for their patients but are worried about malpractice lawsuits. To protect themselves they order many unnecessary tests, procedures and pills.

(3) Patients don't care about the cost of all those tests, procedures and pills as long as their insurance company is paying.

The market for buying and selling health care is broken. This market failure is not the fault of our doctors. It is the result of a poorly designed system with too much concentrated power and inadequate regulation. The "proof" that free enterprise can deliver desirable outcomes assumes free and equal information. It breaks down in the presence of special "insider" information such as that held by the medical establishment. Solving this problem is not easy, but the first step is to fully understand the problem.

Economic theory has traditionally assumed that all parties to a transaction have equal information. In an auction, the seller and bidders have pretty much equal information about the item being auctioned off. In 2001 George Akerlof, Michael Spence and Joseph Stiglitz won the Nobel Prize in Economics for showing that asymmetric information can distort markets and result in market failure.[6] The out-of-control costs of our current health care system provide a prime example of market failure due to (among other things) asymmetric information.*

The classic example of symmetric versus asymmetric markets is the new car market versus the used car market. For our immediate purpose, we can substitute the health care market for the used car market to obtain an analogous comparison. A new car salesman would probably not try to convince you to buy a new car by telling you that if you fail to act today, your old car might fall apart at any moment. You obviously know more about your old car than the new car salesman does so there's no point in that strategy.

---

* See report from UK Office of Health Economics, 12 Whitehall, London at http://oheschools.org/ohe.pdf

(11.) HEALTH POLICY

But what about your body? After all sorts of tests and procedures, the medical establishment knows more about your body than you do. Who are you to object to whatever they say you need? It is far from a normal economic market. With little private or public oversight, costs can get out of control really fast.

What about the recalcitrant patient who is unwilling to go along with unneeded pills, procedures and doctor visits because of the cost? Remember that the objective of the current health care system is to maximize the profits of the medical establishment in order to maximize the frequency and amount of their campaign contributions.

The way to solve the *recalcitrant patient problem* is to make sure that each patient has health insurance. That way, patients don't have to pay directly so they have nothing to lose except their time in going along with all the extras. Health insurance with no deductible and no co-pay serves to *anesthetize* the patient to ever higher health care costs.

What about all those television ads for every kind of drug imaginable? Are we being talked into drugs we don't really need or aren't really all that effective? President Eisenhower warned us about the military-industrial complex, but what about the medical-pharmaceutical complex? Does the prescription drug system go too far in transferring power to the medical establishment?

In summary health care costs are out of control resulting in "market failure" because: (1) Politicians are motivated to set up a system that maximizes the power of the medical establishment at the expense of everyone else; (2) Doctors are motivated to order all sorts of unnecessary tests, procedures and pills; (3) Patients are motivated to cooperate as long as it is all paid for by insurance. After all, it's all "free"!!!

Make people pay extra for their bad health habits

If you were upset by the prospect of government "death panels" deciding whether you should live or die, perhaps you will also be upset by a panel of experts deciding what you should eat. Should Congress impose special taxes on unhealthful foods?

Congress has failed to get at a root cause of our rising health care costs. We must confront obesity and unhealthful eating to save lives and cut costs. Our health problems break down into three types: (1) Unlikely problems you don't anticipate; (2) Problems you expect but can't do much about; (3) Problems you could have prevented or greatly reduced the probability of.

Everyone agrees we should pay for insurance for Type One problems. Most people agree with paying for Type Two. But why should we all have to pay for Type Three?

Some people take wild and reckless chances with their health. They expose themselves to all sorts of dangers, eat lots of unhealthful things and avoid exercise. To make matters worse, once covered by health insurance, they do even more unhealthful things.** This last bit is what economists call the "moral hazard" of insurance. Moral hazard simply means that you increase the risky behavior you are insured for just because you have

---

** Even people without health insurance drive up our health care costs by frequently showing up at emergency rooms in hospitals where our laws require that they be given emergency care. Many such emergencies such as heart attacks and strokes are preventable.

insurance.[7] This also applies to any situation where you know that your health care will be paid for by someone else regardless of your unhealthful behavior.

A basic principle of economics is that you pay for what you get. The costs are directly associated with the corresponding benefits. In principle, insurance deviates from this only in the sense that the premium you pay should be directly associated with the expected benefit rather than the actual benefit. If your house is more expensive to replace or you live in a more tornado-prone area, you will have to pay a higher premium for home insurance.

Health insurance follows this same basic principle for Type One problems, which are essentially just bad luck. Type Two problems can be foreseen but are uncontrollable, such as a gene that puts a woman at high risk for breast cancer. Here many of us would agree to redistribute the costs of this type of misfortune. It's not her fault. She was born that way. Give her a break.

The real issue is with Type Three. These people could have prevented or at least reduced the probability of health problems. But they didn't. Worse yet, many of them increased their unhealthful behavior, taking advantage of the rest of us and making us pay. This moral hazard problem violates the principle that you pay for what you get. It is a key source of our rising, out-of-control health care costs.

This has nothing to do with some nanny state trying to tell you how to live your life. We don't care if you want to smoke like a fiend, drink yourself into a stupor and eat greasy burgers, fatty foods and sugary snacks like there's no tomorrow. (Actually some of us do care, but that's not the point.) We just don't want to pay for your unhealthful behavior.

Conservatives (not to mention liberals) have to face the fact that someone has to pay if we are going to have health insurance (either public or private). If the word "taxes" is too upsetting to our Tea Party friends, just call it a "premium adjustment."

We need to call upon a panel of medical experts to construct a list of unhealthy foods.[8] There could be several categories from extremely bad to just plain bad. We need to apply the "premium adjustment" (aka federal sales tax) to these foods and other unhealthy consumables.[9] It may not be feasible to determine how much exercise you're getting or how recklessly you drive your car, but we certainly can do something about all the bad food you eat, which is driving up our health care costs.

Now is the time to impose a federal sales tax on unhealthful food.[10] To compensate the poor and reduce calories, food stamps should count double when purchasing unprocessed fruits and vegetables.

Congress must pass a health insurance law that gets at this root cause of our rising health costs.

To some libertarians even private health insurance is a bad idea

Not everyone without health insurance is poor. Some are young libertarians who, like a number of younger folks, think they're invincible (probably the same ones texting while driving). Libertarians don't want government or other authoritarian entities controlling their lives.

A libertarian might define "government" as a collective entity that collects taxes (or insurance premiums) and set rules and regulations about what they can and cannot do. In this sense your health insurance card is like a government ID card. It doesn't really matter to some libertarians whether the "government" is called Medicare, Humana or Blue Cross Blue Shield, it's just one more entity trying to control their lives.

To most people, going without health insurance is a game of Russian roulette. To a young libertarian, buying health insurance is like buying a lottery ticket. Statistically, buying a lottery ticket on average produces a negative return. No government or private entity would run a lottery if it didn't make money from the average player. The insurance industry operates the same way.

Let's do the math. If you were to survive 30 years without health insurance, what difference would it make? Let's say your health insurance premiums were a flat $500 a month for 30 years. Instead, if you were to save that and invest it compounded monthly at an annual interest rate of 3 percent, 5 percent or 8 percent, how much would you end up with? The answer is: $292,097, $417,863 or $750,148, respectively. (See formula below.)

Alternatively, you might get into a terrible car accident or inherit a debilitating disease, lose your job and your home and end up on the street. My grandfather said "insure against those things that would dramatically upset your life, but not against things you could cover out of your bank account." I assumed this meant I should get health insurance with an appropriate deductible.

What should the average person do? A statistician has been defined as a person who can put her left hand in

---

$500 invested each month for 30 years and compounded monthly:

$$\text{Value of investment} = \$500 \sum_{j=1}^{360}\left(1+\frac{r}{12}\right)^{j}$$ where r is the annual interest rate.

freezing water and her right hand in boiling water and say, "On average I feel just fine." If you can "feel just fine" under such circumstances then maybe you don't need health insurance, but for the rest of us, health insurance is a necessary expense to avoid a potential disaster.

Will public-option health insurance doom us to a life of socialism?

Socialism is defined as government ownership of the means of production, but the term is often used to refer to government control in general. Recently the prospect of government control of health insurance has become a contentious issue. Such a prospect is not as new or as dangerous as some people claim. Americans have been living with various forms of socialism for many years.

Elderly on Medicare and Social Security are not the only ones living with socialism in this country. In most urban communities if there is a fire in your home, you call the socialist fire department. If someone tries to break in, you call the socialist police department.[11]

Why are there few, if any, book rental companies in America? That would be because of all those socialist libraries. Most people got their education in socialist elementary and secondary schools. Let's not forget all those socialist roads and bridges and that socialist military that some of us have served in. Then there's that socialist worker who drops off the mail at your home six times a week. Is it time to stop the spread of all this socialism?

A close relative called me the other day gravely concerned about the rush toward socialist medicine. Her favorite talk radio show has been expounding on the evils of socialism again. She seemed beside herself with worry. I tried to calm her fears by pointing out that as a retiree she is already under socialized medicine. As a county social worker she spent her life as a socialist worker directing her clients to various county socialist services.

Conservatives and liberals have one thing in common. They are both worried about an evil authoritarian entity controlling them and exploiting them. For conservatives, it's big government. For liberals, it's big business. There is something about fear that causes careful, logical analysis to fly out the window. Reforming health insurance will require a great deal of thought and hard work by the moderate middle. It's much easier to take things to extremes and talk in slogans, but it's not likely to lead to an optimal solution for a very complex problem.

Some people claim that even a small public option alternative health insurance program will inevitably lead to a complete government takeover of health insurance. In general, do public companies crowd out private ones? The history of the Brazilian economy is one where a substantial number of public companies successfully competed side by side with private ones for many decades.[12] In many places such as Eastern Europe and China, private companies have been crowding out unprofitable public ones. There is nothing inevitable about a public company crowding out a private one or vice versa. It all depends on the nature of the market and the rules of the game.[13]

Consider how public and private companies have fared in America in the past. The post office dominated the mail delivery service until recent years when UPS and FedEx among others have taken over a great deal of the more profitable business and are gradually crowding out the public option, which is constrained by the political necessity of providing home delivery to every citizen. The public library has prevented the development of an extensive book rental market, but, so far, has not done much to deter private DVD rental businesses like Blockbuster and Netflix (although digital downloads could change that before long).

Throughout American history, private schools have competed with public schools. Public education has certainly not crowded out private education. If anything it is public tax-supported education that is on the ropes and in danger of losing out more and more to its private competitors.[14]

Private security services have maintained a strong presence in the commercial security business while the public law enforcement has focused on the equal application of the law to rich and poor alike. Even our military use some private armed security contractors. Volunteer fire services generally only operate in smaller, rural communities and private fire protection services of an emergency nature are not really viable for protecting the general public. Tax-supported public fire departments play a vital role.[15]

The general conclusion is that the picture is very mixed with the socialist approach sometimes dominating and sometimes only filling in with necessary, but unprofitable, community services. The bottom line is that effective and fair competition is essential to controlling costs. If we are serious about introducing competition in health care, all providers of medical services should be required to post their prices before any service is performed. The real threat to our health care system is not socialism, but inadequate transparency and the lack of competition among health care providers.

Any health insurance system should be designed to maintain as much competition as possible with effective incentives to drive down costs while achieving key goals such as universal coverage (analogous to the post office's universal delivery) and no rejection for pre-existing medical conditions. Left-wing and right-wing slogans will not solve this problem. Only a carefully designed, comprehensive health insurance system will fill the bill.

Obama health care plan failed to fully address the perverse fee-for-service incentive system

At the beginning of the health care debate, President Barack Obama promised to reward doctors and dentists for better outcomes instead of the number of procedures performed.

When this debate began, he emphasized the importance of changing the perverse fee-for-service incentive structure in our health care system, which currently pays many of our doctors and dentists per procedure rather than by salary or by successful health care outcome per dollar of health care expenditure. At the beginning of the health care debate the Obama administration pointed to this incentive structure as the primary cause of our runaway health care costs.[16]

The only change to incentives in the health care law passed by Congress came in the form of some restrictions on a patient's right to file a malpractice lawsuit. This change does not help the patient directly, although it may reduce the incentive for doctors to order some unnecessary tests.

When insurance companies fully cover health care costs with small deductibles and co-pays that are not sensitive to actual prices per procedure, then health care costs will continue to rise. Hospitals and doctors must be required to inform patients in advance and in writing of the costs of each procedure. Patients should be encouraged to shop around for high quality health care at a reasonable price.

Until our perverse health care incentive system is changed in this country, we will continue to find that patients will be further exploited by a system designed to maximize profits whether outcomes for patients are good or bad. Neither the Republicans nor the Democrats in this debate have adequately addressed this fundamental perverse incentive system. Until they do, health care costs will continue to rise rapidly and improvements in patient health per dollar of cost will not improve significantly.

Asymmetric information leads to market failure in dentistry

Dentistry is one profession that clearly needs reform. Anecdotal evidence suggests a range of prognoses based on the same set of dental X-rays. Some dentists may be too conservative in their treatment while others may go well beyond what's necessary. Repaying mortgages and loans for dental equipment can put some dentists into financial difficulty with the rest of us. This is aggravated by a cutback in the demand for cosmetic procedures during recessions and the limits insurers place on dental fees. Under such circumstances some dentists may find themselves desperate for additional cash. No matter how much time and effort you put into taking good care of your teeth, it won't matter if your dentist has decided to give you a few more crowns, needed or not.

(11.) HEALTH POLICY

Almost all dentists have honest intentions, but some get carried away with "preventative" procedures that are not needed. State dental boards are designed to police the dental practice to protect the public. Sometimes dental fraud is discovered and the convicted dentist is held to account. An ABC News investigation in 2008, "Drilling for Dollars,"[17] reported unnecessary fillings, root canals and even jaw surgery. It is not clear whether this reveals the full extent of the problem or just the tip of the iceberg. Is the DNA of a dentist so different from that of a mortgage banker so as to make a dentist immune from excesses? After all they are both "just trying to help people."

Getting a second opinion is costly because it usually requires getting an additional set of X-rays. Too-frequent exposure to X-rays has been linked to cancer. Even if the proposed treatment is expensive, it is usually at least partly covered by insurance. This coverage further reduces the incentive of the patient to get a second opinion.

As Cass Sunstein and Richard Thaler demonstrated in their book *Nudge*[18] and Malcolm Gladwell showed in his book *Tipping Point*,[19] small changes can make a big difference. A small change might substantially reduce dental costs.

The 2001 Nobel prize in economics was awarded for revealing the distortions that emanate from markets with asymmetric information — markets in which at least one party to a transaction has more information than the others. As it turns out, dentistry is a prime example. Dental patients are not trained to read their own dental X-rays.

The asymmetric information problem in dentistry can be easily corrected. At about 10 cents per patient, dentists could be required to give their patients a copy of their X-rays on a CD every time new X-rays are taken, regardless of whether the patient requests them. This "nudge" might just motivate a patient to get a second opinion.

There may even be a way to get a second opinion for less money. With luck, every good dentist at some point will reach retirement age. With sufficient demand and easy access to a patient's dental X-rays, retired dentists could offer to review a patient's X-rays and provide a second opinion for a fee. With digital X-rays this could even be done over the Internet. Patients can then send their X-rays by e-mail (or regular mail) or hand carry them to their favorite retired dentist to get a second opinion. In some cases, a follow-up physical exam may also be needed.

Requiring dentists to give each patient a copy of their dental X-rays on a CD could help discourage dental fraud, reduce unnecessary dental procedures and expenses, help protect the reputation of the dental profession and give retired dentists a little extra income.

State dental boards have been created to protect the public and the reputation of the dental profession. The official state dental board websites are www.pr.mo.gov/dental.asp for the state of Missouri and www.kansas.gov/kdb/ for Kansas. Find out how to contact the dental board in your state. To help protect the public and the dental profession's reputation, report any suspicious cases to your state dental board such as at dental@pr.mo.gov or info@dental.state.ks.us. Similar websites can found for other states.

12. Personal Health:
weight loss and weak bones

The first two selections introduce some novel ideas. The No-Eat-Day Diet is a controversial approach to both weight maintenance and slow, consistent weight loss over time. It is designed for people who have trouble motivating themselves to lose some weight or at least avoid gaining weight. It takes into account the problem of overcoming your body's *set point*, the weight your body tries to maintain in spite of your efforts to change it. The calorie restriction method in the second selection is just as controversial as the first. It proposes calorie restriction as a possible strategy for reducing the likelihood of developing cancer. As with the No-Eat-Day Diet, more research is needed to confirm this proposal.

The third selection introduces some humor. As with the first selection, it involves devising incentives to motivate your weight loss. It essentially asks why it is that terrorists can manage to motivate themselves to commit a suicide bombing for some misguided cause, but we can't seem to motivate ourselves to lose a few pounds. It includes some specific suggestions for weight loss which lead naturally to the fourth selection, which outlines a health plan for living longer.

The fifth and sixth selections are all about enhancing bone density and avoiding osteoporosis. While weight-bearing exercise is a well-known strategy for avoiding bone loss, the newer low-acid eating strategy needs careful consideration. It may be the answer to why Americans who consume more calcium than just about any other people on earth have a considerably higher rate of bone fractures than Asians, who are often lactose intolerant and consume much less calcium. The answer may be that the traditional Asian low-protein diet produces much lower blood acid levels than the American high-protein diet. High blood acid leaches calcium right out of our bones. Americans may be pouring more calcium into the bathtub, but our high-acid eating is leaving the tub unplugged so much of the calcium we're consuming is going right down the drain. Low-acid eating plugs the drain.

The final two selections consider decisions we make about how often we see our doctor and the quality and quantity of food we consume. Are we always rational in our choices or do we make more irrational choices than traditional economic theory would predict? Sorting out our rational from our irrational behavior and then developing the discipline to convert the irrational back to the rational could greatly improve our health outcomes.

The No-Eat-Day Diet:
A good strategy or bad advice?

The objective of the No-Eat-Day Diet is to never have a no-eat day. Some people believe that fasting no more than once a month may cleanse the body of toxins. Other people think that it is a bad idea in principle. This presents them with a paradox. Ironically the No-Eat-Day Diet works best for people who object to a day of fasting because they will be more motivated to never have to go through one. It works well for weight maintenance, but can also be used to lose weight slowly over time.

Here's how it works. You set a maximum weight you don't want to exceed (a number at or just above your current weight). Every time you lose a few pounds, you can lower this maximum by a pound. You then weigh yourself every morning. If your weight exceeds your maximum, then it's a no-eat day. On a no-eat day, you eat nothing, but instead drink a big glass of water at each meal and, probably, take your normal medications, if any. Check with your doctor.

Most diets have difficulty moving your body's natural set point – the weight your body tries to maintain from day to day. Cutting back a little doesn't move your set point. You must let your body know in no uncertain terms that you want your set point moved lower.

The diet is primarily for weight maintenance, but also could be used to nudge down your weight over time. If you get hungry, just take a walk, take a nap, work out at the gym or do whatever works as a distraction.

No-eat days are tough. You don't want to ever have to go through one. But that's the point. If you are careful, you never will. On a big-eat day you may have to help your body return to its set point. Had a big lunch? Skip dinner. Planning a big dinner? Skip lunch. Do whatever it takes, but know that the numbers don't lie. You will be facing the scale in the morning.

Is calorie restriction a good defense against cancer?

Various studies have suggested that calorie restriction may work to extend life.[1] If you eat less, can you avoid cancer and live longer?

Previous research carried out with mice has demonstrated that calorie restriction can improve both health and longevity. A more recent study on rhesus monkeys has confirmed these results. The mice and the monkeys significantly reduced the diseases usually associated with old age, including cancer.[2]

In response to these and other similar research studies, some people have undertaken calorie restriction as a way to protect their health as they get older and to live longer. It is important to point out that this refers to intentional weight loss. Unintentional weight loss in seniors has been associated with an increased probability of dementia and mortality.

Some people who believe in this theory claim that calorie restriction can reduce your probability of getting cancer. Your body can do three things with calories: (1) supply immediate energy for physical activity, (2) help to maintain or replace the cells you've got, and (3) expand by growing more cells. Cancer involves uncontrolled rapid cell growth. Your body can use a number of things to facilitate rapid cell growth: (a) refined sugar, (b) high cholesterol foods that are designed specifically to support rapid cell growth (e.g. egg yolks), (c) other foods that supply extra calories beyond those needed just to maintain or replace your body's existing cells.

This theory claims that when you restrict these and related items you restrict rapid cell growth and, therefore, limit the spread of cancer. If you limit your calories so your body only gets enough calories to maintain current physical activity and defend what you've got, then, according to this theory, not enough calories are left over to support rapid cell growth, and you inhibit the spread of cancer. Calorie restriction may prevent cancer from getting sufficient critical mass to overcome your body's natural defenses. It may trigger a change in metabolism analogous to that of a bear going into hibernation.

There may be at least one drawback to take into consideration. If your weight drops considerably, your bone density may decline as well. Thin people should consider weight bearing exercise and low-acid eating (e.g. eat raisins) to avoid osteoporosis.[3] Suffering a hip fracture can significantly reduce life expectancy.

Only a carefully designed health strategy can make it possible to avoid both cancer and osteoporosis to maximize your chances of a long and healthy life.[4] As yet no studies of the effects of intentional calorie deprivation have been carried out on humans. Consequently, whether calorie restriction should be part of a sensible health strategy is still unclear. What is clear is that a lot more research needs to be done.

Reprogram your subconscious mind to commit terrorism or lose weight

Why is it that some people can motivate themselves to commit a suicide bombing for some completely wrong-headed cause, but you can't motivate yourself to lose weight?

Why wait for someone to come along to brainwash you? Why not take control and brainwash yourself? Don't rely on the latest fad diet. Create your own plan to take responsibility for your own body. Take control and reprogram your subconscious mind.[5]

Your subconscious mind is the realm of your core beliefs and the source of your instinctive reactions. It is nothing more than the accumulation of what you tell yourself every day (internal messages) and what others tell you (external messages). It is programmed by repeatedly feeding it essentially the same message over and over again. Every time you say, "Math class is boring," you are programming yourself for failure. Every time you say, "I know I can learn Spanish," you are programming yourself for success. External messages such as "God is great" and "death to America" or "Tide clean" and "Ford tough" help program your subconscious mind.[6]

A new second lieutenant had just started at the battalion headquarters at Fort Knox where I worked as a clerk. He had just gotten married. Every day he had something bad to say about his wife, such as "She burned the toast." A year later he got divorced. No surprise. He programmed himself for that divorce.

The first thing to do to program yourself for a suicide bombing, or for weight loss, is to surround yourself with propaganda. Yes, you need to subscribe to all those weight-loss magazines. No, you should not be listening to all those "foodie" programs on the radio or watching them on television. What about all those friends of yours? Think of three possible groups of friends you could have: (1) Friends who want you to commit terrorism; (2) Friends who will support you no matter what you do; and (3) Friends who will nag you to death if you don't lose some weight. Now if you are serious about losing weight, which group of friends do you want to associate with?

What about that food you are bringing home? Did you know that some of it is "illegal." Yes, it's the food that tastes really good. Forget ice cream, but maybe you could get away with some no-sugar-added fudge bars. They taste okay, but not good enough to cause you to break training between meals. For a between-meal snack, those salty peanuts are just too addictive; how about some unsalted walnuts? Forget potato chips and cookies, they are totally "illegal." Remember, if it tastes too good, you don't want it in your house.

To lose weight, avoid anything that contains a lot of sugar and salt. Sugar is sneaky since it comes disguised in so many forms like high-fructose corn syrup and the like.[7] Processed foods tend to have too much sugar and salt. It is better to make meals from scratch. It is hard to find canned soup without lots of sodium. It's much better to make your own soup. Same thing with salad dressing -- just mix some garlic and lemon juice with some olive oil to create a tasty salad dressing without sugar, salt or preservatives.[8]

It is not necessary, nor desirable, to avoid salt altogether, especially if you sweat a lot in hot weather. Even if you try, you will still almost certainly get more salt than you need. To avoid excess salt, you could look for low-sodium or no-sodium foods, but check with your doctor first. Since many foods don't have a reduced sodium version, it pays to check the milligrams of sodium on the label. Is it under 200 mg for a half-cup serving or under 50 mg for 2 tablespoons? When it comes to dodging the deadly bullet of sodium, there is no substitute for doing the math. Medical studies have reported that sodium could thicken and harden your arteries, causing your blood pressure to rise, which can lead to a heart attack or stroke.[9]

The most critical part of programming yourself for weight loss is recording your weight on a calendar each morning when you arise. If you and your partner do this then you can support one another in your collective weight-loss effort. If you can start each day discussing your weight-loss strategy for the day with your partner, your chances of success are great. Plan ahead by making a light lunch to compensate for that big restaurant dinner you have scheduled. If you overeat at lunch, plan to have just a cup of fruit for dinner.

If you will be attending a reception where you have no control over the food that will be available, decide *in advance* what type of food you will be willing to eat. Eat at home as much as possible, but if you do go out to eat, avoid those all-you-can-eat buffets, which put your wealth strategy (get the most for your money) in direct conflict with your health strategy.

The most important thing to remember is this: You, and only you, decide what to put in your mouth. If you can't control what you put in your mouth, then you can't control anything. Before you try to gain control of anything else in your life, you should first gain control of your weight.[10]

P.S. If you can do one thing for your children to ensure that they have a bright and successful future, teach each of them to gain control of their subconscious mind.

Why healthy living didn't protect Bill Clinton's heart

Former President Bill Clinton was doing everything right. He ate healthfully and got plenty of exercise, yet he had more cholesterol buildup in his arteries. What went wrong?

Clinton's primary problem might not be cholesterol, but homocysteine. The old cholesterol theory is gradually giving way to the homocysteine theory. If your arteries are smooth, the level of bad cholesterol in your blood might not matter. With smooth arteries, that bad cholesterol might not collect along your artery walls. On the other hand, substantial homocysteine damage to the walls of your arteries could allow even small levels of bad cholesterol to build up rapidly.

The source of Clinton's problem may be those industrially produced cookies, crackers and traditional fast foods that he consumed earlier in his life. They often contain partially hydrogenated oils and transfats. Those oils and fats transformed the essential amino acid methionine in Clinton's blood into homocysteine. Then the homocysteine went to work damaging his artery walls.

According to the homocysteine theory, the old bad Bill Clinton, who ate all that junk food, is causing the new good Bill Clinton, who eats right and exercises every day, to have to pay for his past dietary misdeeds.

Clinton could have blocked the creation of homocysteine by eating lots of dark green, leafy vegetables and other sources of B-vitamins, which turn homocysteine back into the otherwise harmless methionine. All he can do now is eat healthfully to avoid additional damage to his arteries. The earlier damage is there, and he must just try to live with it. Perhaps his artery walls will gradually repair themselves over time.

The primary proponent of the homocysteine theory is Kilmer S. McCully, M.D., who wrote *The Heart Revolution: the extraordinary discovery that finally laid the cholesterol myth to rest and put good food back on the table.*

If you don't want to put all your eggs in one basket and commit yourself to either the cholesterol theory or the homocysteine theory, you can always play all sides against the middle by lowering your bad cholesterol, eating lots of green, leafy vegetables and avoiding all those transfats and partially hydrogenated oils.

Men in their 70s must be defensive players

Senator Edward Kennedy's death was unusual. Brain cancer strikes only about 7 people per 100,000 per year, with over a third surviving at least five years. It is impossible to know if Kennedy could have done anything to avoid brain cancer since each death is unique, but his death reminds us once again how vulnerable men in their 70s are. In general men who want to make it out of their 70s and into their 80s must become defensive players. Here's the game plan:

(1) Unless you sweat a lot when the weather is hot, avoid salt. It takes a while for your taste buds to adjust, but reducing sodium intake not only lowers most men's blood pressure but also slows down the hardening of their arteries. Sometimes this is reflected in the difference between your systolic and diastolic blood pressure numbers. If the difference is growing larger you could be in trouble. A small gap means your arteries are flexible and able to keep a relatively constant pressure, while a larger gap implies that they are stiff and unyielding.[9]

(2) Avoid sugar. This is difficult to do but well worth the sacrifice if you want to make it to your 80s. Sugar is calorie dense and leads to obesity. Sugar also supports rapid cell growth, which is what cancer is all about. When cancer tries to gain a foothold in your body, it is best to avoid food and drink that support rapid cell growth. Babies need rapid cell growth. Old folks not so much.

(3) Avoid transfats. These are the worst kinds of fats that can show up in everything from crackers to french fries. Transfats are associated with partially hydrogenated oils that turn methionine into homocysteine, which can damage the walls of your

arteries. You can reverse this process and convert the dangerous homocysteine back into harmless methionine by eating lots of dark green, leafy vegetables containing B vitamins. Many otherwise transfat laden foods can be made without transfats. Some cities have banned trans fats from restaurants, forcing many fast food companies to get rid of them.

(4) Avoid saturated fats. These raise your bad cholesterol which clogs your arteries. Red meat, french fries and many other popular foods typically contain a lot of saturated fat. Consuming saturated fats significantly raises your probability of having a heart attack or stroke.

(5) Eat lots of fruits and vegetables. Buy them raw and unprocessed with no sugar or salt added. Fresh or frozen are better than canned. Avoid overcooking in water. Better to briefly steam vegetables or eat them raw. Make your own tomato sauce heated with a little olive oil to enhance lycopene production, which helps protect the prostate.[8]

(6) Unless you are already thin, lose weight. Being thin seems to be almost a requirement for entry to your 80's and 90's. Bug and animal studies have shown that calorie deprivation triggers some sort of defensive mechanism in the body that protects it from all sorts of age-related diseases.

(7) Exercise, exercise, exercise. Vigorous aerobic exercise helps the heart while weight-bearing exercise protects your bones. Exercise gets your blood flowing to all parts of your body, flushing out potential carcinogenic toxins that might otherwise do you harm. Enjoy walking or running in the great outdoors or use a treadmill and/or exercise bike in the winter. Swimming is great for your heart, but careful, consistent weightlifting can strengthen your bones.

Life has many milestones. For most people, graduating from high school and making it into their 60s are not too difficult. Getting into one's 70s is a bit harder. Making the grade to graduate into your 80s or 90s takes a lot more work and determination. Good luck.

Bone density and osteoporosis

The mistrial concerning claims that Merck's anti-osteoporosis drug Fosamax allegedly weakens jaw bone tissue reminds us of the rather complicated issues many older people face in dealing with bone density problems. By some estimates, half of all women and one third of all men over 65 will develop bone density problems.

While the Fosamax lawsuit involved only jaw bones, more general allegations suggest the possibility that bisphosphonates like Fosamax may not simply slow the loss of old bone but may also inhibit the formation of new bone. So far such claims do not appear to be supported with sufficient evidence.

Aging generally leads to weaker bones. For young people, the renewal process of new bone replacing old bone keeps up at a relatively even pace at least until somewhere around age 30 to 35. Unfortunately as one ages, the pace of new bone creation declines while old bone destruction continues at the previous rate.[11]

Some of this gap is an inevitable aspect of aging while some may be due to the tendency of older people to cut back on tasks involving physical exercise. This is especially true for people who had physically demanding jobs who do not replace their work activity with equally demanding physical activity in retirement.

A simple heal test may provide the first indication of trouble. A more extensive (and expensive) body scan from the neck through the hips can provide a more comprehensive and reliable reading. A T-score of -1 means your bone density is one standard deviation below normal. T-scores between -1 and -2.5 indicate osteopenia. T-scores below -2.5 indicate osteoporosis. A T-score of -2.5 corresponds to a bone density two and a half standard deviations below normal.

Scientific research has shown that bones under stress grow faster than those not subject to stress. This use-it-or-lose-it situation means that a lack of weight-bearing exercise can lead first to osteopenia and eventually to osteoporosis. This problem may be worse for those who have lost a great deal of weight as they have become older. It is one of the few drawbacks to weight loss for older Americans.

The ideal solution to this problem for older Americans is to take up weight-bearing exercise of some sort. Filling coat pockets with rocks or other heavy weights before going for a walk may be helpful. Taking up weight lifting may also be effective. This is especially important for those wishing to avoid the side effects and expense of drugs. If you can't find a weight-bearing exercise that is sufficiently effective to stop or reverse your bone loss, you may want to consider talking to your doctor about taking a drug to increase your bone density.

The ideal bone density drug would be one that would increase the rate of new bone creation to bring it back to where it was in your youth. Unfortunately, at the time of this writing the drugs generally available on the market are designed to simply slow down the loss of old bone. Throughout your life your body replaces old bone with new bone for a reason. Over time the old bone deteriorates and needs to be replaced with new bone. A drug that only causes your body to hold onto old bone without increasing the rate of formation of new bone is not ideal. It would be much better if a drug could be created to stimulate the creation of new bone instead.[12]

Cytokine-6 is the chemical that our bodies generate to get rid of old cells (old bone). A substantial increase in cytokine-6 causes a large amount of cytokine-10 to be produced, which is the chemical responsible for cell repair and growth (new bone). Without exercise, not enough cytokine-6 is produced to trigger cytokine-10 production. A drug that suppresses the production of cytokine-6 might also prevent cytokine-10 production. Loss of old bone is slowed but the production of new bone may stop.[11]

Calcium has been deemed essential for strengthening bones. Vitamin D is needed to assist in the absorption of calcium. For men, some studies have found an association between high levels of calcium and prostate cancer. However, no causal link has been established. Perhaps too much calcium leaves insufficient vitamin D for the needs of the prostate. A lot more research is needed to figure out exactly what is happening.[4]

Bone density is not the only issue here. Bone density is like cement in a column holding up a building. It needs to be reinforced with steel rods, which in the case of bones is the cellular matrix that acts as a structure around which the bone grows. A cement column without steel reinforcement can collapse in an earthquake. Bone density is important but not sufficient. If your cellular matrix is not strong as well, then you may break a hip or spine even with good bone density. Weight-bearing exercise is key to maintaining a strong cellular matrix.

If after consulting with your doctor you decide to take a drug to try to reduce your bone loss, you should realize that the cost of such drugs varies widely. You can save a lot by getting a generic version of the drug if it is available. In some cases you can cut the cost of a dozen bone preserving pills from around $350 to just over $12 by thorough and systematic comparison shopping.

Why cavemen didn't have weak bones

In their new book *Building Bone Vitality*,[3] Amy Joy Lanou and Michael Castleman point to research suggesting that excessive consumption of high-protein foods produces too much acid in our blood that in turn leaches calcium from our bones. Weak bones in men are a relatively new problem. Cavemen did not have this problem.

We all need to consume a reasonable quantity of protein for growth, including bone growth. However, too much protein accompanied by too few green leafy vegetables can cause bone problems. Protein metabolizes as acid in our blood while fruits and vegetables generally metabolize as alkaline bicarbonate. Too much acid without enough alkaline could lead to osteoporosis. Eating dried fruit such as raisins can help counteract high levels of acid in the blood.

In his 2008 book *In Defense of Food*,[13] Michael Pollan deplores the fact that not only are we not eating enough unprocessed fruits and vegetables, but we are getting our protein from animals that got to eat very little, if any, grass and were fed mainly with grains. He points out that this doesn't generate the right nutrients in the meat we eat. It produces a quality of meat that is nutrient poor relative to what our ancestors ate. This change has not helped us in our struggle to maintain strong bones.

Our bodies are constantly working to break down old bone and replace it with new bone. Both protein and non-protein food sources are needed to get the right balance for this bone destruction and bone creation process to work smoothly. The missing ingredient that makes this all work properly is weight-bearing exercise. Heavy exercise triggers a burst of cytokine-6 production which tears down old bone which, in turn, triggers cytokine-10 production which builds up new bone.[11]

A low-acid diet is not likely to be sufficient to maintain strong bones if not accompanied by weight-bearing exercise. Bones deteriorate naturally over time if left to themselves. Our ancestors performed lots of hard physical labor. Until after the industrial revolution, there was no time to sit around and watch tv especially since there was no tv to watch anyway. People typically spent all day working in the fields.

In ancient times cavemen had to chase their sources of protein around the plain and through the forest. They also had to be able to run fast to avoid getting eaten themselves by ubiquitous predators. Cavemen didn't have to worry about developing weak bones. They never got to stop running long enough to develop them.

Should you be required to see a doctor once a year?

Should your health insurance company require you to see a doctor at least once a year? Would such a requirement decrease or increase diseases and preventable deaths? The answer may be more complicated than you think.

(12.) PERSONAL HEALTH

Doctors are busy people. They have to be because our fee-for-service system means they have no salary and get paid only by the number and nature of the patient visits and procedures. The *no patients means no money* part of the equation makes sense. But what about the *lots of patients means lots of money* part? What if some patients are really sick and can't get their doctor's full attention because they are in and out in 10 minutes?

What happens in the typical check-up visit? The nurse records your weight and height and takes your blood pressure. The doctor places a stethoscope on your chest and back, has you breathe deeply and then asks if you have any unusual pains or discomfort. That's nice, but you can record your weight every day at home, and every pharmacy in town has a blood pressure testing device (not to mention the $15 one you can purchase to use at home). As to your lungs, most people know right away when their lungs aren't performing up to par.

Have you discovered that your doctor didn't have time to review your test results before seeing you or doesn't get to all the items on the list of reasons for seeing him or her that day? The problem is called Taylorism.[14] It is an inherent part of capitalism and the industrial revolution. It is as American as apple pie.

Taylorism refers to the ideas of industrial engineer Frederick W. Taylor in his 1911 book *Principles Of Scientific Management*. Basically Taylor emphasized the importance of assembly line efficiency to maximize profits. Time is money. On an assembly line, maximum productivity is essential. The quicker an item can be processed, the fewer labor hours required, and the higher the profit.

To some extent voluntary methods to increase the throughput in the medical production line have been successful. Allowing the pharmaceutical companies to advertise on television was a brilliant move for bringing in more patients. It was clearly a win-win deal for both the drug companies and the doctors.

A friend of mine asked me the other day how I was paying for all my meds. To his surprise I said, "What meds?" Could a 65-year-old man actually be drug free? After all, those nice old people in television commercials are all on drugs so why not me? Since these are mainly prescription drugs, seeing a doctor is the only legitimate way to get the drugs. Of course, renewing your prescription will require some more medical tests. As long as the drugs don't actually cure you, but just manage your real or imaginary condition, this medical version of Taylorism works really well.

But, alas, Taylorism is not satisfied with business as usual. Labor productivity must be continually enhanced. This means speeding up the production line some more. In medical terms this means processing more patients with more drugs, tests and procedures more quickly. In all fairness to doctors, the exorbitant money sometimes awarded in malpractice lawsuits motivates doctors to order testing and drugs at the drop of a hat. If a patient mentions a drug they might need (one they presumably heard about on television), doctors feel pressured to prescribe it just to avoid the possibility that failure to do so will set the stage for a nasty lawsuit if the corresponding disease or illness develops.

What this all boils down to is a very sick system. Patients who need lots of attention just slow things down. Unless they have lots of their own money or lots of insurance money, they aren't going to get all the help that they need. The system is just not designed to focus on the few patients who really need a lot of attention. Unless doctors are put on salaries and a cap is put on malpractice awards, we're not going to see any improvement any time soon.

Perhaps there are some intelligent prevention measures that insurance companies should require in order to reduce your premiums -- like a colonoscopy at least once every 5 or 10 years. Requiring annual doctor visits doesn't necessarily make sense if the goal is to reduce the overall incidence of disease and preventable death. Let those who really need to see a doctor get all the time and attention they require. The rest of us can decide for ourselves as to whether we need help checking our height, weight, blood pressure and lungs on an annual basis.

Irrational behavior exposes flaw in economic theory

When the holiday season approaches, we remind ourselves once again to avoid overeating at all those holiday parties and family gatherings. Inevitably we will fail miserably in our attempts at self-restraint. Perhaps it is not ourselves, but economic theory that fails us.

After our recent recession it has become obvious that traditional economics with its assumption of rational behavior hasn't worked. Despite Adam Smith's famous scenario in his 1776 book *An Inquiry into the Nature and Causes of the Wealth of Nations*[15] about the benevolent compatibility of human nature and market forces, economic theory as revealed in the housing and financial markets has let us down. What is not so obvious is that we violate that same economic theory every time we skip exercising and wolf down that extra serving of ice cream and cake.

Economic theory assumes not only rationality, but also consistency, which implies self-discipline in pursuing one's self-interest. Failure to adhere to these assumptions at the microeconomic level can lead to disaster at the macroeconomic level as we have recently seen.

When facing physical demands such as agreeing to exercise or declining sweet desserts at some date in the future, people will insist that they are determined to maintain discipline, only to frequently give in to temptation when the day arrives. Does this reveal irrationality, inconsistency or just a failure to act in one's own long-term self-interest?

In his 2008 book *Predictably Irrational,*[16] Dan Ariely reports the results of experiments where he required students in some of his classes to hand in three papers at evenly spaced intervals while in other classes students were allowed to set their own deadlines or simply hand in all three papers at the end of the term. The results were not surprising. Students required to meet the evenly-spaced deadlines wrote much better papers on average than those who chose a less rigid schedule.

Providing students with structure may enhance learning, but professors are leery of providing it. Professors have an incentive to avoid requiring class attendance and giving lots of homework with deadlines since, *ceteris paribus*, such requirements will reduce a professor's score on the teacher-course evaluation forms that the students fill out at the end of the course and that are so important for a professor's tenure and promotion.

This reveals a problem with traditional economic theory. Rationality and consistency in pursuing one's own self interest appear to require an amount of self-discipline often not forthcoming from many, if not most, people. Incentives are not there to help people stay on track.

Economics fails because people fail. A good theory should be able to describe and predict behavior. Making assumptions that don't work does not provide a solid foundation for a good theory. Saying *"The theory hasn't failed. It's people who failed."* doesn't cut it. A theory that describes hypothetical people in a hypothetical world is not what we need.

When economists came to recognize market failure in the past, they incorporated it into the theory by calling for corrective policies. When the existence of *negative externalities* in the form of excessive pollution were revealed, economists proclaimed that the private cost to polluters was lower than the total cost to society so pollution taxes must be imposed on polluters to make up the difference.

How does this apply to your caving in to your cravings at the last minute in spite of your good intentions? Behavioral economists have now developed a concept they call *internalities*.[17] Your short-term self fails to fully appreciate the long-term costs of your short-term behavior. This means that you are exhibiting *negative internalities*. The long-term costs need to be more effectively incorporated into your short-term calculations.

So where does the theory of ice cream and cake behavior lead? How does such behavior at the micro level affect macro policy? The answer is simple. Obesity at the micro level leads to obesity at the macro level.[18] We are becoming one fat nation. Our health care bills are out-of-control. We are heading for bankruptcy at the individual level and at the national level.

Under this new approach to economics, policies are needed to provide incentives to get our short-term self to recognize the goals of our long-term self and to get us to more fully appreciate the long-term costs of our bad behavior. Trying to fix the problem at the national level is just playing around with the symptoms of the problem. What we really need are policies that help us skip the ice cream and cake and get back on the treadmill.

13. Future World:
DNA, nanotechnology, ocean ocean living, Internet advertising and shopping

This last chapter is a roller coaster of wild and crazy thinking. No one really knows for sure what the future will really look like, but it is fun to speculate. Anticipating possibilities can give us a heads-up in some situations where our investments of time and mental energy may pay off in preparing for a bizarre future world. Some older folks may tend to discount all this because they don't expect to be around for any of it. However, the world is changing faster than many people realize so it may be prudent to ponder these possibilities to avoid too much future shock.

In the first selection, we start out in Wal-Mart with relatively tame suggestions for new technology to enhance the shopping experience through the use of electronic shopping lists and gift lists. Price comparison software is essential to an efficient, competitive market and to provide significant savings for consumers. Computer programs can optimize your entire shopping trip.

The second essay stretches the imagination a bit more. The electronic ink t-shirt would allow more individuals to participate in advertising as they go about their daily chores. Ads would be remotely delivered and targeted specifically for location, time of day and the people around you.

The problem of dealing with all that land under our oceans is discussed in the third selection. With more countries making undersea claims for oil and mineral rights, the problems of undersea development and ownership are not that far off. The United Nations needs to agree on some rules for undersea territories before things get out of hand.

The fourth and fifth selections get at what it means to be human. Ready or not, the whole question of whether and how to duplicate, not just clone, human beings needs to be addressed. It may seem far-fetched, but many things we take for granted now were not possible a hundred years ago, such as air travel and cell phones that can instantly call just about anywhere on earth. There is an old mantra that Larry Page at Google likes to say: "Have a healthy disregard for the impossible." The sixth selection extends these ideas to altering the DNA of household pets to allow them some degree of speech capability. Would you like your dog to talk?

The final selection is the most far out of all. It anticipates a time when nanotechnology will enable us to transcend physical barriers and, as the old telephone advertisement says, "Reach out and touch someone."

(13.) FUTURE WORLD

Stores like Wal-Mart need shopping list reminder boxes

Have you ever arrived home from a shopping trip to Wal-Mart and discovered you forgot to buy an item or two? Would you like know what your kids and your spouse want for their birthday or holiday gifts? It might all be made much easier if you had a quick way to create a list at home and print it out at the store.

If you're an unemployed computer programmer, here's a job for you. Impress your friends and family by creating the next really cool app. This is how it works. Create an app that allows consumers to edit their shopping list from their home computer or mobile phone. Then create a small, simple, brightly-colored, in-store box where customers can scan their credit card and get an immediate print-out of either their regular shopping list or their gift list for free. Using your credit card as ID is just to avoid the need for a keypad and to save time.

Now create a Facebook or LinkedIn app that interfaces with your in-store app to allow selected friends and family to provide gift suggestions for themselves and others.[*] Why struggle to think up gifts to buy if you can get others to do it for you?

This is just the first step down a revolutionary path that will connect your refrigerator, pantry and storage areas directly to the items on the shelves as you walk down store aisles.[1] Tiny devices behind each item's label will communicate with your home computer to compare what you've got with your preferred inventory.[2] Any shortfall will automatically be added to your shopping list.

---

[*] See Facebook applications: MyRegistry.com, Wishlist Butler, WISH LIST, etc

In the not-too-far-off future, you may carry a key fob with a tiny scanner so you can scan the SKU number** off an item of interest to transmit to your own shopping or gift list or to the list of a friend or family member. Since the key fob is connected remotely to your home computer via the cell phone in your pocket or purse, it could vibrate gently if you are passing by an item you meant to add to your shopping cart.[3]

Your home computer will be able to combine the pricing information from your credit card purchases and general pricing information off yet-to-be-created product pricing websites similar to gasbuddy.com to allow you to see how much you paid for each item in the past and what the prices are at various stores now.[4]

The hot new computer apps will solve a simple version of what is known in statistics as the "traveling salesman" problem. It will tell you, given the price of gas, distance between stores and your car's miles per gallon, what items to purchase in which stores and in what order to minimize your time and maximize your savings.[5]

Make money just by wearing an electronic ink t-shirt

Amazon's Kindle exploits electronic ink for the first time in a big way. Now it's time to use the MIT Media Lab's invention for something even more fun. Just wear your electronic ink t-shirt around town to earn money.

As far as I know, E Ink Corporation hasn't caught on to this idea yet, but here's how it would work. E Ink Corporation or any other company licensed by E Ink to use its technology would produce a t-shirt with a

---

** See Android phone applications: Compare Everywhere and Shop Savvy.

lightweight, flexible, electronic ink, removable panel attached to the back with Velcro. (Optional magnets would be available to attach panel to the side or rear of your car.) It also would include a GPS locator and wireless Internet connection that attaches to the panel and fits in your pocket.

You buy one of those E ink t-shirts and go to an Internet advertiser's website to register as a publisher[6] just as you would to sign up to allow their ads to display on your own website. Companies go to an Internet advertiser's website and bid for space to advertise their products. The advertiser sends out signals to various t-shirts around town advertising the product. The display on the back of the t-shirt gives the website for ordering the product.[7]

You just wear your t-shirt around town. If you're a sports fan, just wear it to the stadium and sit in a front row seat. If anyone orders the product from a mobile device with a GPS locator that has passed within 30 feet of you in the last 15 minutes, then the advertiser is paid by the company and, in turn, gives you some of that money. Even without a GPS, it takes only three cell phone towers to triangulate a location. Alternatively, instead of giving the product's website, the ad could give a unique discount code to provide when buying the product. This would allow local retailers without websites to advertise.

Naturally, this would work only for certain types of products and businesses, so the advertiser would need to be selective. Ads could be targeted depending on where you happen to be located around town at the time. The advertiser would have to be sure not to send the same ad to two t-shirts in the same location to avoid a payment conflict.

Okay, there have been some crazy ideas over the years. Some have worked out and others have not. First remember that Postmaster General around 1950 who said, "In 10 years we'll have rocket mail to Japan." Then there was the guy who claimed you would be able to take a heavy steel and glass vehicle loaded down with people, run it along a special road at a high speed, and it would suddenly rise up into the air and land in the New York area two and a half hours later. Now he was really crazy!

You'd have to be a Harry Potter fan to believe in that stuff. Next thing you know, someone will want to put gliding wheels and flashing lights on your kids' sneakers.

Forget Mars, there's plenty of land under our oceans

Unhappy with American politics? Looking to start your own country? There's plenty of land under the oceans. We just need to extract oxygen from water and use tightly sealed vehicles and housing.

They'll start out as undersea "cottages" for wealthy people, featuring glass domes in areas with exotic fish and providing a "cool" getaway for those bored with their 60-foot yachts. As these rich enclaves grow, so will the political implications of their existence.

Vladimir Putin sent two special Russian submarines under the Arctic Ocean to claim undersea territory and plant a Russian flag.[8] Canada, Norway and other countries claimed the same underwater land. With two-thirds of our planet underwater, the fight over who owns what has just begun.

The best case scenario is that the United Nations will find a way to get all nations to agree on a common set of rules for territorial rights under our oceans.[9] Over the years the nations of the world have worked out the U.N. Convention on the Law of the Sea.[10] Nonetheless, it may turn out that devising the technology to allow humans to live underwater will be easier than getting the nations of the world to agree on undersea territorial rights. Some of the underwater land may need to be set aside to serve as international parks collectively owned by the United Nations. Such an international park system would be analogous to our national park system.

Once we have agreed on how to allocate land under our oceans, how will that affect our sea lanes and the rights of ships to traverse the globe? Undersea farms are sure to need some "breathing room" above them to avoid crop damage. Why shouldn't undersea countries have the same "overflight" rights as land-based ones?

What about undersea vehicles? What sort of highways will we need to build under our oceans? Short hops between undersea towns and villages are one thing, but if you plan to go any distance, a quick shot up to the surface may provide a faster way for greater distances -- in pressurized compartments, of course.

The demand for new underwater vehicles will provide new sales for GM, Ford, Toyota, et cetera. With global warming melting all the icebergs, a number of the world's communities won't even have to move to take advantage of the new underwater technologies. Russian and American experts need to work together to establish standards for undersea vehicle portals just as they have done with the International Space Station.

Just in case our superhero President, who seems to already be speeding through an enormous agenda, runs out of problems to solve, why not plan ahead a bit?

Stem cells and nanosurgery may change what it means to be human

Stem cells are prompting ethical debates, but a bigger debate is looming. Nanotechnology, which is just beginning to make its debut, may change what it means to be human.

We have recently developed a rather versatile and sensitive artificial hand for amputees. This follows similar improvements in artificial knees, ankles and hips. Is this just the beginning of a long-term trend to replace damaged or aging body parts? Can nanotechnology accelerate this process?[11]

Can we do anything to enhance our brains? Brain scanning experiments have led to a better understanding of the functioning of our brains. We can see how the two hemispheres of our brain interface with one another. Information is flowing back and forth that may initially allow us to record the physical manifestations of our thinking process and ultimately allow us to intervene to retrieve or add to specific thoughts. This opens up the possibility of adding to our memory's storage capacity. Combine pattern recognition using artificial neural networks[12] with relational databases[13] and Google search technology[14] and what do you get? => Technology to potentially help enhance brain power and retrieve information more efficiently.

Is it time to ask where all this is leading? Could we ever get to the point where it might be possible to replace the entire body? Will nanotechnology lead to nanosurgery? What if nanosurgery ultimately allows us to transfer the mind out of the brain into silicon in a stainless steel model? We could then avoid cancer, heart attacks and strokes. Will a timely transfer to a bionic body save our Medicare system from paying for the costs of old age?

Of course you would want to have more than one copy of your mind in case you get hit by a truck. You can't expect to live forever if you don't back up the backup that backs up the backup.

At this point you may have already concluded that the only one who has lost his mind is me. But consider how often we have been proven wrong in the past. At first people thought the world was flat. Sailors and astronomers together proved that one wrong. In Galileo's day most people believed that the sun revolved around the earth. Before 1903 who would have thought that a heavy glass and metal vehicle filled with overweight people could go speeding down a special road and suddenly rise into the air and land in the New York area in two and a half hours?

Einstein was reported to have said, "God doesn't play with dice," but modern physicists in quantum mechanics have shown randomness[15] to be an integral part of reality. In the 1960s some people thought space travel to be purely science fiction and the Apollo moon landings to be a ruse filmed in Hollywood. Most people still believe that there are only four dimensions, but some modern string theorists claim that there are actually 11 dimensions.[16]

You may think this is all ridiculous, but if you are getting older, it might not hurt to place an advance order with Microsoft or Apple for one of the first stainless steel models of your body, just in case. It may turn out that only taxes are inevitable.

Three rules for dealing with backup copies of your brain?

Stem cells are leading to the reproduction of body parts.[17] We are approaching the point where we might be able to make a spare copy of your liver, kidney or heart. The wonders of medical science never cease.

What about the brain? What if we are able to reproduce your brain? First we must ask what it means to reproduce your brain. Unlike any other organ, your brain contains a vast array of information that is being continuously updated moment by moment.[18] We would have to capture its content at a particular moment in time.

Creating a second copy of your brain presents some serious problems. We need to understand those problems and devise some rules in advance to mitigate them.

Let's say you're a bit of a paranoid and want a copy of your entire body, including your brain, ready to go in case you have a fatal accident. To keep your new body and brain up to date, you would need it to be alive to receive updated information. With two brains operating at the same time, certain legal issues arise. Who owns your house? What if your new brain decides to sell some of your stock or wants to sleep with your spouse? It could all get very confusing. Consequently, we have our first rule.

> Rule #1: Only one copy of a person's brain may be active at any point in time. Any backup brain or brains must be kept in suspended animation.

This naturally raises a new problem. What if you promise something and then die before updating your new brain? Is your new brain responsible for any promises made by your old brain for the period after the duplicate was made? What if your old brain commits murder after creating your duplicate? Should your new brain be held responsible for something it had no control over or knowledge of and could not have stopped? This leads to our next rule:

Rule #2: The information necessary to create a new brain must be updated continuously and the new brain must not be created from that information until the exact moment the old brain expires.

This second rule requires constant scanning of your brain with wireless transmission of the information to some Internet storage location to keep it up to date. The time gap between when your old brain was last scanned and your new brain is created must be kept as small as possible.

All this leads to a third problem. Wouldn't the complete backup of your body and brain lead to a moral hazard problem. You now are free to engage in all sorts of risky behavior knowing that you have a backup. People might drive their cars at amazing speeds with lots of smashing and crashing in multi-car pile-ups. As with many moral hazard problems, this one generates what economists call *negative externalities*.[19] Others have to pay the price for your bad behavior. Consequently, we have the third and final rule.

Rule #3: Persons engaging in risky behavior must pay substantially higher premiums as well as higher brain storage and backup fees than their risk-adverse colleagues.

Planning ahead by instituting these three rules will help make things go more smoothly for a brighter future for all of us.

Altering animal DNA:
Would you like your dog to talk?

We've been altering plant and animal DNA indirectly for decades with cross-germination[20] and cross-breeding.[21] We've produced crops that are disease and drought resistant and chickens with breasts so big they are almost too top heavy to walk.

Is it time to go one step further and directly change the DNA of our pets and wild animals?

Some American zoos borrow giant pandas from China. Why don't they just breed their own? The problem is that panda fertility rates are very low. China's Beijing Genomics Institute in Shenzhen has mapped the DNA of pandas. Should we just alter the DNA of pandas to make them breed a bit more like rabbits? What about those rabbits? How about all those pesky deer and squirrels over-running our urban areas? Should we alter their DNA to breed less?

Ready or not, the science of creation is moving ahead at a rapid pace. Before long we may be facing some fairly serious questions about how far we should go in altering existing creatures or creating new ones.

When it comes to DNA, mice and humans are quite similar.*** It turns out that about 85 percent of the 30,000

***Information about comparing mouse and human DNA sequences can be found at www.ensembl.org.

genes from mice and men match. With chimpanzees and humans, the match appears to be at least 95 percent.

For some key gene sequences, animals and humans have the same genes, but a different subset of those genes is turned on. This is the problem of epigenetics, which focuses on understanding which genes are actually turned on and why.[22]

Over time environmental factors and social circumstances can alter the expression of existing genes. This may well be the case in the sexual behavior of bonobos,[23] which are pygmy chimpanzees. They live only in the Congo River Basin. They use sexual favors for everything from greeting other bonobos to settling disputes and trading for food. (See National Geographic for more on bonobos.) While some of this may be learned behavior, some may be more deeply rooted in their genetic expression.

Radical changes in the look, capability and behavior of animals may well just turn out to be a matter of turning on or off existing genes rather than adding or subtracting genes. Teaching lions and tigers to eat vegetables may require only a few adjustments to their DNA.

Now we have to face the tough questions. What if scientists figure out how to alter the DNA of dogs to allow them to talk? Perhaps we could make some modifications to the vocal cords and voice box with a few minor adjustments to the mouth and jaw. Do you want a dog that talks? What if your neighbor's dog can talk and yours can't? Would that make your dog inferior? Wouldn't such a handicap be unfair to your dog? Surely this will make dog shows more interesting. Imagine Fido reading poetry to win a blue ribbon.

With genetically modified corn and chickens too top heavy to walk, some think that the world is already becoming a scary and crazy place. Don't worry; it will be getting a lot more crazy and a lot more scary before long.

If your friends don't answer their cell phones, just give them a nanonudge

Ever use that virtual "poke me" tool in Facebook? One day you will be able to give a friend enjoying their latté at a café halfway around the world a real nanonudge. (Yes, a real physical nudge.)

Christopher Columbus was using the only means available in 1492 to try to get a message to China. Almost 375 years later in *The Great Tea Race of 1866*,[24] getting a message from Fuzhou in China to London in the UK still took over three months (102 days to be exact).[25] Back then a cell phone call or an email message was unimaginable.

In nanospace there can be seemingly vast relative distances between nanoparticles in a granite rock. You could send a nanobot through a granite rock without touching another particle. Just send your nanobot through the center of the earth. All that super hot lava is no problem for your superfast nanobot. A tiny GPS locator will guide the way.

If you can do that, then surely you can send a physical nanonudge from your apartment in NYC to your boyfriend hanging out with his pals at that café in Beijing.

Ever see those swarms of birds flying together in formation? They swirl up and down and all around in seemingly endless patterns with no apparent purpose. Now imagine zillions of nanobots doing the same thing.

(13.) FUTURE WORLD

Einstein said that an object's mass becomes very big as its speed approaches the speed of light. A nanoparticle is so small that it could reach great speeds without attaining excessive mass. Nanobots could not only move through mountains but actually move mountains. If the CIA had nanobots in October 1962 during the Cuban Missile Crisis, they could have taken the cigar right out of Fidel Castro's mouth.

Nanotechnology offers us amazing precision and incredible power. The Russians know it. They are working hard to understand, develop, master and control nanotechnology. Russia has hosted conferences for experts on nanotechnology to make sure that it is staying ahead of potential competitors in this field.

The United States got a jump on nuclear power because one physicist went to visit Einstein to ask him to write to President Roosevelt about the possibility of creating an atomic bomb.[26] Peaceful use of nuclear power was just an afterthought.

Nanosurgery will be just one of a vast array of benefits that come from understanding and controlling nanotechnology.[27] We can either develop nanotechnology now, or wait and ask permission from the Russians to work on it later.

P.S. Think about the Internet, airplanes, television, atomic bombs, artificial hearts, cell phones, email, travel to our moon or to Mars, et cetera. From the vantage point of the 18th or 19th centuries, they are all so . . . . . not possible. Moreover, if there really are 11 dimensions as string theorists claim, then nanotechnology is small potatoes on the list of things we don't understand.

References*

Chapter 1: Energy Policy

[1] Wald, Matthew L. "A nuclear critic draws a lesson from France's success." *New York Times*– Energy and Environment Blog. January 19, 2010.

[2] Lucas, Paul. "Brazil hits 10 million flex-fuel mark." *Green Car Website.* March 9, 2010.

[3] Staff Writer. "On track for 2012 wind power goal." *Reuters News Service.* March 13, 2010.

[4] Sorkin, Andrew Ross (editor). "Another Big Ethonal Maker Flames Out." *New York Times* – Business Dealbook Blog. April 8, 2009.

[5] Posner, Richard A. "The Robinson-Patman Act: Federal regulation of price differences." Vol. 131 of *AEI Studies*. American Enterprise Institute for Public Policy Research. 1976.

[6] Levy, Michael. "Why $30 a barrel oil could save lives, bring democracy to Iran and end the war." *News Blaze* (Op-Ed) commentary. July 10, 2009.

[7] Sobel, Dava. *Longitude: the true story of a lone genius who solved the greatest scientific problem of his time.* Penguin Books. 1995.

[8] Korosec, Kirsten. "Big ethanol's lobbying investment of 2010: tax credits and tariffs." *BNET Energy.* February 17, 2010.

[9] Phillips, David. "Murphy Oil expanding ethanol footprint: if price is right." *BNET Energy.* February 3, 2010.

[10] Levine, Michael; Mark Roe. "How to make a petrol tax politically viable." *The Financial Times.* Tuesday, July 7, 2009.

Chapter 2: 21st Century Challenges

[1] Handoyo, Stefan S. "The cause of the next global recession." *The Jakarta Post.* Monday, March 1, 2010.

[2] Andrade-Cetto, Juan; Joaquin Filipe; Jean-Louis Ferrier (editors). *Selected papers for the international conference on informatics in control, automation and robotics 2008.* Springer-Verlag. 2009.

[3] Gelman, Andrew. *Bayesian Data Analysis.* Chapman and Hall/CRC Press. 2004.

[4] Bhidé, Amar. *The Venturesome Economy.* Princeton University Press. 2010.

[5] Leitman, Seth; Bob Brant. *Build your own electric vehicle.* McGraw-Hill. 2009.

---

* Note: All footnotes and endnotes are presented in *Emeritus Style*.

[6] Kaplan, Siena; Rob Sargent. *Plug-in cars: powering America toward a cleaner future*. Environment Texas Research and Policy Center. January 2010.

[7] Patterson, Scott. *The Quants: how a new breed of math whizzes conquered Wall Street and nearly destroyed it*. Crown Publishing Group. 2010.

[8] Ohsawa, Yukio; Katsutoshi Yada. *Data mining for design and marketing*. Chapman and Hall/CRC Press. 2009.

[9] Li, Xue; Shuliang Wang; Zhao Yang Dong (editors). *Advanced Data Mining and Applications*. Springer-Verlag. 2005.

[10] Packard, Vance. *The Hidden Persuaders*. David McKay Company. 1957.

[11] Packard, Vance. *The Status Seekers*. David McKay Company. 1956.

[12] Galbraith, John Kenneth. *The Affluent Society*. Houghton Mifflin Company. 1958.

[13] Mays, Elizabeth (editor). *Credit risk modeling: design and application*. Glenlake Publishing Company. 1998.

[14] Wong, Stanley. *Foundations of Paul Samuelson's Revealed Preference Theory*. Routledge. 2006.

[15] Segaran, Toby. *Programming Collective Intelligence*. O'Reilly Media Inc. 2007.

[16] Bell, R.; J. Bennett; Y. Koren; C. Volinsky. "The Million Dollar Programming Prize." *Spectrum* (IEEE). Vol. 46(5). May 2009, pp. 28-33.

[17] Hurrell, James W.; Harry Van Loon. "Decadal variations in climate associated with North Atlantic oscillations." *Climate Change*. Vol. 36(3-4). July 1997.

Chapter 3: Education

[1] Flynn, James R. "The mean IQ of Americans: massive gains 1932 to 1978." *Psychological Bulletin*. Vol. 95(1). January 1984. pp. 29-51.

[2] Flynn, James R. "Massive IQ gains in 14 nations: what IQ tests really measure." *Psychological Bulletin*. Vol. 101(2). March 1987. pp. 171-191.

[3] Anderson, Charlie. "Young web pioneer is an old hand." *Kansas City Business Journal*. March 24, 2006.

[4] Ip, Kwan Fun; Christian Wagner. "Weblogging: a study of social computing and its impact on organizations." *Decision Support Systems*. Vol. 45(2). May 2008. pp. 242-250.

[5] Kaufman, Scott Barry. "Are you smarter than Aristotle?: on the Flynn Effect and the Aristotle Paradox." *Psychology Today* – Beautiful Minds Blog.

[6] Cole, Michael; Karl Levitin; Alexander Luria. *The Autobiography of Alexander Luria*. Lawrence Erlbaum Associates. 2006.

[7] Beattie, Alan. *False Economy: A Surprising Economic History of the World.* Penguin Books. 2010.

[8] Tough, Paul. *Whatever It Takes: Geoffrey Canada's Quest to Change Harlem and America.* Houghton Mifflin. 2009.

[9] Abrevaya, Sandra (contact). "Secretary Duncan releases application for $650 million to support innovation." *U.S. Dept. of Education* – Press Release. March 8, 2010.

[10] Hawkes, James S. *Adventures in Statistics.* Quant Systems. 1992.
  Hawkes, James J.; James S. Hawkes; William H. Marsh. *Discovering Statistics.* Hawkes Publishing. 2004.

[11] Marsh, L.C.; K.L. Wells. "Key aspects of a computerized statistics course." *Journal of Computing in Higher Education.* Vol. 8(2). Spring 1996. pp. 72-93.

[12] Davenport, Thomas H.; Jeanne G. Harris. *Competing on Analytics:The New Science of Winning.* Harvard Business School Press. 2007.

[13] Levitt, Steven D.; Stephen J. Dubner. *Freakonomics.* HarperCollins. 2005.

[14] Merrigan, Court. "The Espresso Book Machine, an ATM for books: Will e-books suffer if it takes off?" *TeleRead.* April 29, 2009.

[15] Staff Writer. "New technology promises to prolong the life of the book." *The Economist.* February 25, 2010.

[16] Tsuruoka, Sonia. "The Notre Dame Postmortem." *Scoop/Daily* (www.scoopdaily.com). May 18, 2009.

Chapter 4: Economic Theory

[1] Marx, Karl; Friederich Engels. "Manifesto of the Communist Party." *The Communist Party Manifesto 1848.* Cosimo Books. 2009.

[2] Pink, Daniel H. *Free Agent Nation.* Warner Books. 2001.

[3] Fukuyama, Francis. *The End of History and the Last Man.* Simon & Schuster. 1992.

[4] Mankiw, N. Gregory. *Principles of Economics.* Cengage Learning. 2008.

[5] Mirowski, Philip. *More Heat than Light.* Cambridge University Press. 1989.

[6] Heufer, Jan. *Essays on Revealed Preference.* Technischen Universität Dortmund. 2010.

[7] Minsky, Hyman P. *John Maynard Keynes.* Columbia University Press. 2008.

[8] Ebenstein, Lanny. *Milton Friedman.* Palgrave MacMillan. 2009.

[9] Ostrom, Elinor. *Governing the Commons.* Cambridge University Press. 1990.

[10] Williamson, Oliver. *The Mechanisms of Governance.* Oxford University Press. 1996.

[11] Heller, Michael. *The Gridlock Economy.* Basic Books. 2008.

[12] Triana, Pablo. *Lecturing Birds on Flying: Can Mathematical Theories Destroy the Financial Markets?* John Wiley & Sons. 2009.
[13] Geanakopolos, John. "Three brief proofs of Arrow's Impossibility Theorem." *Economic Theory.* Vol. 26(1). July 2005. pp. 211-215.
[14] Smith, Adam. *An Inquiry into the Nature and Causes of the Wealth of Nations.* Printed for Thomas Dobson, at the stone house in Second Street. 1789.
[15] Hirsch, Fred. *Social Limits to Growth.* Harvard University Press. 1976.
[16] Taleb, Nassim. *The Black Swan: The Impact of the Highly Improbable.* Random House. 2007.
[17] Ariely, Dan. *Predictably Irrational.* Harper-Collins. 2009.
[18] Camerer, Colin F.; George Loewenstein; Mathew Rabin (editors). *Advances in Behavioral Economics.* Princeton University Press. 2004.
[19] Schwartz, Barry. *The Paradox of Choice.* Harper-Collins. 2004.
[20] Brafman, Ori; Rom Brafman. *Sway: The Irresistible Pull of Irrational Behavior.* Random House. 2009.
[21] Ubel, Peter. *Free Market Madness.* Harvard Business Press. 2009.
[22] Kinsley, Michael. *Creative Capitalism.* Simon & Schuster. 2008.
[23] Lo, Andrew; Craig MacKinlay. *A Nonrandom Walk Down Wall Street.* Princeton University Press. 1999.
[24] Shermer, Michael. *The Mind of the Market.* Henry Holt and Company. 2008.
[25] Paley, William. *Natural Theology.* R. Faulder. 1802.
[26] Francis, Keith A. *Charles Darwin and the Origin of Species.* Greenwood Press. 2007.
[27] Hollander, Samuel. *The Economics of Thomas Robert Malthus.* University of Toronto Press. 1997.

Chapter 5: Economic Policy

[1] Staff Writer. "How to redeem California IOUs (registered warrants)." www.mymoneyblog.com. September 2009.
[2] Staff Writer. "Bank of America, Wells Fargo and Citibank to accept California IOUs as deposits." Americanbankingnews.com. September 2, 2009.
[3] Petruno, Tom. "Bank of America sets cutoff for redeeming California IOUs." *Los Angeles Times* at Latimes.com. July 3, 2009.
[4] Brown, Ellen. "How California could turn its IOUs into dollars." www.webofdebt.com. June 22, 2009.
[5] Quint, Thomas; Martin Shubik. "An elementary discussion of commodity money, fiat money and credit." Cowles Foundation Discussion Paper No. 1460. April 2004.

[6] Grunwald, Michael. "Person of the Year 2009: Ben Bernanke." *Time Magazine* at www.time.com. December 16, 2009.

[7] Isidore, Chris. "Geithner under fire." Money.cnn.com. November 30, 2009.

[8] Hagstrom, Robert G. *The Warren Buffett Way*. John Wiley & Sons. 2005.

[9] Staff Writer. "The charticle McCain doesn't want you to see." http://gawker.com/5059089/. October 4, 2008.

[10] Frank, Robert H. *Falling Behind*. University of California Press. 2007.

[11] Kibbe, Mathew B. "The minimum wage: Washington's perennial myth." *Policy Analysis*. Cato Institute. May 23, 1988.

[12] Chapman, Jeff. "Employment and the minimum wage: evidence from recent state labor market trends." *Economic Policy Institute Briefing Paper No. 150*. May 11,2004.

Chapter 6: Research Methods

[1] Arnold, Lutz G. *Business Cycle Theory*. Oxford University Press. 2002.

[2] Friedman, Milton. *The Optimum Quantity of Money*. Transaction Publishers. 2007.

[3] Multiple Authors. "System Dynamics." *Wikipedia*. November 2002 to March 2010.

[4] Radzicki, Michael J. *Foundations of System Dynamics Modeling*. Sustainable Solutions, Inc. 1997.

[5] Smith, H.C. *The Illustrated Guide to Aerodynamics*. TAB Books. 1992.

[6] O'Neill, Ian. "The 'Mars Curse': why have so many missions failed?" www.universetoday.com. March 22, 2008.

[7] Malkiel, Burton G. "The efficient market hypothesis and its critics." *Journal of Economic Perspectives*. Vol. 17(1). Winter 2003. pp. 59-82.

[8] Bernanke, Ben S. "On Milton Friedman's ninetieth birthday." www.federalreserve.gov. November 8, 2002.

[9] Aharony, Joseph; Itzhak Swary. "Contagion effects of bank failures." *The Journal of Business*. University of Chicago Press. Vol. 56(3). 1983. pp. 305-322.

[10] Anderson, David R.; Dennis J. Sweeny; Thomas A. Williams. *Statistics for Business and Economics*. Thomson/South -Western. 2008.

[11] Wu, Hulin; Jin-Ting Zhang. *Nonparametric Regression Methods for Longitudinal Data Analysis*. John Wiley & Sons. 2006.

[12] Greene, William H. *Econometric Analysis*. Pearson/Prentice Hall. 2008.

[13] Staff Writer. *Vensim*. Ventana Systems. 1995.

[14] Karris, Steven T. *Introduction to Simulink*. Orchard Publications. 2008.

[15] Hickmann, Meredith A.(editor). *The Food and Drug Administration*. Nova Science Publishers. 2003.

[16] Morgan, Stephen L.; Christopher Winship. *Counterfactuals and Causal Inference*. Cambridge University Press. 2007.

[17] Rosner, Bernard. *Fundamental of Biostatistics*. Duxbury. 2006.

[18] Matthews, John N.S. *Introduction to Randomized Controlled Clinical Trials*. Chapman & Hall/CRC Press. 2006.

[19] Department of Biostatistics, University of Kansas Medical Center, http://biostatistics.kumc.edu.

[20] Soong, Seng-jaw. http://faculty.dom.uab.edu/sjsoong.

[21] Jaccard, James; Robert Turrisi. *Interaction Effects in Multiple Regression*. Sage Publications. 2003.

Chapter 7: Foreign Affairs

[1] Moyo, Dambisa. *Dead Aid*. Farrar, Straus and Giroux. 2009.

[2] Hubbard, Glenn; William Duggan. *The Aid Trap*. Columbia University Press. 2009.

[3] Morrison, Wayne M. "China-U.S. Trade Issues." Congressional Research Office. September 17, 2009.

[4] Polk, William R. *Understanding Iran*. Palgrave-Macmillan. 2009.

[5] Anderson, Kaila. "Free market meets altruism in Kiva." *The Orange County Register*. March 12, 2010.

[6] Moyo, Dambisa. *Dead Aid*. Farrar, Straus and Giroux. 2009.

[7] Staff Writer. "The Dutch Disease." *The Economist*. November 26, 1977.

[8] Associated Press. "Tons of food aid rotting in Haiti ports." *Barbados Free Press*. March 7, 2008.

[9] Hubbard, Glenn; William Duggan. *The Aid Trap*. Columbia University Press. 2009.

[10] World Bank. *Doing Business 2010* (annual report). Palgrave-Macmillan. 2009.

[11] Riccardo, David. *The Principles of Political Economy and Taxation*. J.M. Dent & Sons. 1911.

[12] Smith, Adam. *An Inquiry into the Nature and Causes of the Wealth of Nations*. Printed for Thomas Dobson, at the stone house in Second Street. 1789.

[13] Maraniss, David. *Rome 1960: The Summer Olympics that Stirred the World*. Simon & Schuster. 2009.

[14] Launius, Roger; John Logsdon; Robert Smith (editors). *Reconsidering Sputnik: Forty Years Since the Soviet Satellite*. Routledge. 2002.

[15] See www.kiva.org or www.rotarianmicrocredit.org.

[16] Chance, Giles. *China and the Credit Crisis*. John Wiley & Sons. 2010.

[17] Hoey, Dennis. "A behemoth finesses its way into port." *Portland Press Herald.* February 17, 2001.
[18] Ferguson, Niall. *The Ascent of Money.* Penguin Press. 2008.
[19] Karabell, Zachary. *Superfusion: How China and America Became One Economy.* Simon & Schuster. 2009.
[20] Turner, John Roscoe. *Introduction to Economics.* Charles Scribner's Sons. 1919.
[21] Boreham, Paul; Rachel Parker; Paul Thompson; Robert Hall. *New Technology @ Work.* Routledge. 2008.

Chapter 8: Terrorism and the Middle East

[1] Dickens, Charles. *The Tale of Two Cities.* Random House. 1950.
[2] Rubens, David. "Umar Farouk Abdulmutallab and the Christmas Day attack: why aren't lessons learned?" Media Consultants. 2009.
[3] Miller, Frederic; Agnes Vandome; John McBrewster. *Fort Hood Shootings.* Alphascript Publishing. 2010.
[4] Tanne, Janice Hopkins. "Killer of Kansas abortion doctor is convicted." *British Medical Journal.* February 1, 2010.
[5] Martin, Gus. *Understanding Terrorism.* Sage Publications. 2010.
[6] Gladwell, Malcolm. *Blink.* Little, Brown and Company. 2005.
[7] Selengut, Charles. *Sacred Fury: Understanding Religious Violence.* AltaMira Press. 2003.
[8] Mahtafar, Tara. "Mojtaba Yahedi: Ahmadinejad-Khamenei rift widening." PBS Frontline. March 14, 2010.
[9] Maslin, Jamie. *Iranian Rappers and Persian Porn.* Skyhorse Publishing. 2009.
[10] House of Commons. "Global Security." The Stationary Office. 2009.
[11] Cimbala, Stephen J. *Shield of Dreams: Missile Defense and U.S.-Russian Nuclear Strategy.* Naval Institute Press. 2008.
[12] Staff Writer. "The Dutch Disease." *The Economist.* November 26, 1977.
[13] Lazzaro, Joseph. "Thomas Friedman: Go green to support Iran's reformers." *Daily Finance.* June 29, 2009.
[14] Gowan, Jackie; Graham Timmins (editors). *Russia and Europe in the 21st Century.* Anthem Press. 2009.
[15] Rose, Charlie. "Benjamin Netanyahu, Prime Minister of Israel." www.charlierose.com/view/interview/10627. September 24, 2009.
[16] Sorensen, George. *Democracy and Democratization.* Westview Press. 2008.
[17] Holder, Benjamin. "Gun Barrel Democracy." *2007 Global Topics.* Vol. 5. Article # 2007-2. Saint Anselm College. 2007.
[18] BBC News Staff. "Iran country profile." BBC News. February 4, 2010.

Chapter 9: Afghanistan

[1] Humayoon, Haseeb. *The Re-Election of Hamid Karzai*. Institute for the Study of War. January 2010.
[2] Pallin, Carolina Vendil. *Russian Military Reform*. Routledge. 2009.
[3] Murphy, Paul. *The Wolves of Islam: Russia and the Faces of Chechen Terrorism*. Brassey's, Inc. 2004.
[4] Baggott, Christopher. *The School of Advanced Military Studies*. SAMS: Fort Leavenworth. 1998.
[5] Adams, Thomas K. "The real military revolution." *Parameters*. Vol. 30. Questia 2000.
[6] Nance, Malcolm. *An End to Al-Qaeda*. St. Martin's Press. 2010.
[7] Dukkipati, Rao V. *Analysis and Design of Control Systems Using MATLAB*. New Age International. 2006.
[8] Heij, C. *System Dynamics in Economic and Financial Models*. John Wiley & Sons. 1997.
[9] Rosser, John Barkley. *From Catastrophe to Chaos*. Kluwer Academic. 2000.
[10] Douglas, Ronald G. *Banach Algebra Techniques in Operator Theory*. Academic Press. 1972.
[11] Gonzalez, Roberto J. *American Counterinsurgency: Human Science and the Human Terrain*. Prickly Paradigm Press. 2009.
[12] Eldridge, Erik B.; Andrew J. Neboshynsky. *Qantifying Human Terrain*. Naval Postgraduate School. 2008.

Chapter 10: Attitudes and Beliefs

[1] Holder, Charles F. *Charles Darwin: His Life and Work*. The Knickerbocker Press. 1891.
  Clayton, Edward T. "The tragedy of Amos "N" Andy." *Ebony*. Vol. 16(12). October 1961. pp. 66-68, 70, 72-73.
[3] Harper, Frederick D.; Marvin P. Dawkins. "The Syphax Child Care Center." *The Journal of Negro Education*. Vol. 54(3). 1985. pp. 438-450.
[4] Reichrath, Jörg (editor). *Sunlight, Vitamin D and Skin Cancer*. Landes Bioscience. 2008.
[5] Holick, Michael F. "Vitamin D: its role in cancer prevention and treatment." *Progress in Biophysics and Molecular Biology*. Vol. 92(1). September 2006. pp. 49-59.
[6] Heber, David; George L. Blackburn; Vay Liang W. Go; John Milner (editors). *Nutritional Oncology*. Academic Press. 2006.
[7] Mukhopadhyay, Carol Chapnick; Rosemary C. Henze; Yolanda T. Moses. *How Real is Race?* Rowman & Littlefield Education. 2007.

[8] Jablonski, Nina G. "The evolution of human skin and skin color." *Annual Review of Anthropology*. Vol. 33, October 2004. pp. 585-623.

[9] Jablonski, Nina G.; George Chaplin. "Skin Deep." *Scientific American*. Vol. 287(4). October 2002. pp. 74-81.

[10] Drew, Elizabeth. *Richard M. Nixon*. Henry Holt/Times Books. 2007.

[11] Ogletree, Charles. *The Presumption of Guilt: The Arrest of Henry Louis Gates and Race, Class and Crime in America*. Palgrave-Macmillan. 2010.

[12] Patrick, Kevin; William G. Griswold; Fred Raab; Stephen S. Intille. "Health and the mobile phone." *American Journal of Preventative Medicine*. Vol. 35(2). August 2008. pp. 177-181.

[13] Nikolaev, Alexander G.; Matthew J. Robbins; Sheldon H. Jacobson. "Evaluating the impact of legislation prohibiting hand-held cell phone use while driving." *Transportation Research Part A: Policy and Practice*. Vol. 44(3). March 2010. pp. 182-193.

[14] Hemenway, David. "Nervous Nellies and Dangerous Dans." *Journal of Policy Analysis and Management*. Vol. 12(2). Spring 1993. pp. 359-363.

[15] Levitt, Steven D.; Jack Porter. "Sample Selection in the Estimation of Air Bag and Seat Belt Effectiveness." *NBER Working Paper*. No.W7210. July 1999.

[16] Heffetz, Ori; Robert H. Frank. "Preferences for status: evidence and economic implications." *Handbook of Social Economics*. July 2008.

[17] McNutt, Patrick A. *The Economics of Public Choice*. Edward Elgar. 2002.

[18] Elias, Stephen; Richard Stim. *Trademark: Legal Care for Your Business and Product Name*. Nolo. 2007.

Chapter 11: Health Policy

[1] Staff Writer. "Unequal information – doctors as agents." Office of Health Economics, 12 Whitehall, London. October 2002.

[2] Marsh, L.; M. McGlynn; D. Chakraborty. Interpreting complex nonlinear models. *Proceedings of SAS Users Group International*. Vol. 19. 1994. pp. 1185-1189.

[3] Chazin, Suzanne. "Is iron making you sick?" *Readers Digest*. October 1995.

[4] Greenemeier, Larry. "Will electronic medical records improve health care?" *Scientific American*. December 1, 2009.

[5] Eddy, David M. "Linking electronic medical records to large-scale simulation models." *Health Affairs*. Vol. 26(2). 2007. pp. 125-136.

[6] Akerlof, George A. *Explorations in Pragmatic Economics*. Oxford University Press. 2005.

[7] Lynch, Wendy D.; Harold H. Gardner. *Aligning Incentives, Information and Choice*. Health as Human Capital Foundation. 2008.

[8] Millwood, Nancy Huehnergarth. "Benefits of a soda tax." *The New York Times on the Web*. January 30, 2010.

[9] Grossman, Michael. "Health benefits of increases in alcohol and cigarette taxes." *British Journal of Addiction*. Vol. 84. 1989. pp. 1193-1204.

[10] Rabin, Roni Caryn. "Nutrition: rise in soda price linked to better health." *New York Times*. March 15, 2010.

[11] Ely, Richard T. *Socialism: An Examination of Its Strengths and Its Weakness, with Suggestions for Reform*. Thomas Y. Crowell & Co. 1894.

[12] Trebat, Thomas J. *Brazil's State-Owned Enterprises: A Case Study of the State as Entrepreneur*. Cambridge University Press. 1983.

[13] Newfarmer, Richard S.; Lawrence Marsh; Lino Moreira. *Employment and Technological Choice of Multinational Enterprises in Developing Countries*. International Labour Office. 1983.

[14] Gouwens, Judith A. *Education in Crisis*. ABC-CLIO, LLC. 2009.

[15] Smoke, Clinton H. *Company Officer*. Thomson/Delmar Learning. 2005.

[16] Halvorson, George. *Health Care Reform Now: A Prescription for Change*. John Wiley & Sons. 2007.

[17] Staff Writer. "Dentists drilling for dollars?" *ABC News*. January 21, 2008.

[18] Sunstein, Cass; Richard Thaler. *Nudge*. Yale University Press. 2008.

[19] Gladwell, Malcolm. *Tipping Point*. Little, Brown and Company. 2000.

Chapter 12: Personal Health

[1] Michels, Karin B.; Anders Ekbom. "Caloric restriction and incidence of breast cancer." *Journal of the American Medical Association*. Vol. 291(10). 2004. pp. 1226-1230.

[2] Weindruch, Richard. "Effect of caloric restriction on age-associated cancers." *Experimental Gerontology*. Vol. 27. 1992. pp. 575-581.

[3] Lanou, Amy Joy; Michael Castleman. *Building Bone Vitality*. McGraw-Hill. 2009.

[4] Gross, Myron D. "Vitamin D and calcium in the prevention of prostate and colon cancer." *Journal of Nutrition*. Vol. 135. February 2005. pp. 326-331.

[5] Sanders, Hugh B. *The Subconscious Diet*. Liberation Press. 2005.

[6] Whyte, Lancelot Law. *The Unconscious Before Freud*. F.Pinter. 1983.

[7] Pollan, Michael. The Omnivore's Dilemma. Penguin Press. 2006.

[8] Whitney, Eleanor Noss; Sharon Rady Rolfes. *Understanding Nutrition*. Wadsworth Publishing. 2010.

[9] Liebman, Bonnie. "Shaving salt, saving lives." *Nutrition Action* (Center for Science in the Public Interest). Vol. 37(3). April 2010. pp. 3-6.

[10] Ferguson, James M.; Cassandra Ferguson. *Habits Not Diets: The Secret to Lifetime Weight Control*. Bull Publishing. 2003.

[11] Henriksen, K.; et al. "Osteoclasts prefer aged bone." *Osteoporosis International*. Vol. 18(6). June 2007.

[12] Gallagher, J.Chris; A.J. Sai. "Molecular biology of bone remodeling: implications for new therapeutic targets for osteoporosis." *Maturitas*. Vol. 65(4). April 2010. pp. 301-307.

[13] Pollan, Michael. *In Defense of Food*. Penguin Books. 2008.

[14] Taylor, Frederick W. *Principles of Scientific Management*. Harper & Brothers Publishers. 1911.

[15] Smith, Adam. *An Inquiry into the Nature and Causes of the Wealth of Nations*. Printed for Thomas Dobson, at the stone house in Second Street. 1789.

[16] Ariely, Dan. *Predictably Irrational*. Harper-Collins. 2009.

[17] Whitman, Glen. "Against the new paternalism: internalities and the economics of self-control." *Policy Analysis*. No. 563. Cato Institute. February 22, 2006.

[18] Acs, Zoltan J.; Alan Lyles (editors). *Obesity, Business and Public Policy*. Edward Elgar. 2007.

Chapter 13: Future World

[1] Symonds, Judith; John Ayoade; Dave Parry. *Auto-Identification Ubiquitous Computing Application*. IGI Global. 2009.

[2] Glielmo, Luigi; Davide Del Cogliano; Corrado De Santis. "System for remotely contolling and monitering a food refrigerator and its contents." *US Patent Application* No. 20090282859. 2009.

[3] Howard-Johnson, Carolyn. *A Retailor's Guide to Frugal In-Store Promotions*. HowToDoItFrugally Publishing. 2009.

[4] Doble, Rick; Tom Philbin. *Cheaper: Insiders' Tips for Saving on Everything*. Random House. 2009.

[5] Coello, Carlos A.; Clarisse Dhaenens; Laetitia Jourdan (editors). *Advances in Multi-Objective Nature-Inspired Computing*. Springer. 2009.

[6] Brown, David J.; Richard Boulderstone. *The Impact of Electronic Publishing: The Future for Publishers and Librarians*. K.G.Saur. 2008.

[7] Leal, Kendra Mae. "Technology: Friend or Foe to the Publishing Industry." Master's Thesis. Pace University. 2009.

[8] Zellen, Bary Scott. *The Geopolitics of Climate Change in the Arctic*. Greenwood Publishing Group. 2009.

[9] Klein, Natalie. *Dispute Settlement in the UN Convention on the Law of the Sea.* University of Cambridge Press. 2009.

[10] United Nations. *Law of the Sea Bulletin.* No. 70. Office of Legal Affairs. 2010.

[11] Popat, Ketul. *Nanotechnology in Tissue Engineering and Regenerative Medicine.* CRC Press. 2010.

[12] Ripley, Brian D. *Pattern Recognition and Neural Networks.* Cambridge University Press. 2007.

[13] Azuaje, Francisco. *Bioinformatics and Biomarker Discovery: 'omic' data analysis for personalized medicine.* Wiley-Blackwell. 2010.

[14] Miller, Michael. *Google•pedia: The Ultimate Google Resource.* Que Publishing. 2007.

[15] Ruvinsky, Anatoly. *Genetics and Randomness.* CRC Press. 2010.

[16] Gubser, Steven S. *The Little Book of String Theory.* Princeton University Press. 2010.

[17] Sherwood, Lauralee. *Human Physiology: From Cells to Systems.* Cengage Learning. 2010.

[18] Brooks, Rodney A.; Pattie Maes. *Artificial Life IV.* MIT Press. 1994.

[19] McConnell, Campbell R.; Stanley L. Brue. *Economics.* McGraw-Hill. 2006.

[20] Ray, P.K. *Breeding Tropical and Subtropical Fruits.* Narosa Publishing House. 2002.

[21] Gillespie, James R. *Modern Livestock and Poultry Production.* Delmar Learning. 2004.

[22] Allis, C. David; Thomas Jenuwein; Danny Reinberg (editors). *Epigenetics.* Cold Spring Harbor Laboratory Press. 2007.

[23] Furuichi, Takeshi; Jo Thompson (editors). *The Bonobos: Behavior, Ecology and Conservation.* Springer. 2008.

[24] Clark, Arthur Hamilton. *The Clipper Ship Era.* G.P. Putnam's Sons. 1911.

[25] Blake, John. *The Sea Chart.* Anova Books. 2009.

[26] Gosling, F.G. *The Manhattan Project: Making the Atomic Bomb.* U.S. Dept. of Energy, January 1999.

[27] Demin, A.V.; G. G. Levin. *Nanoelectronics and Nanophotonics at the First International Forum on Nanotechnologies.* Vol. 52(6). 2009. pp. 683-686.

237

Index

A

Abdulmutallab, Umar Farouk ·
136, 137, 138, 232
Abouhalkah, Yael · 249
Abrevaya, Sandra · 228
Acs, Zoltan J. · 236
Adams, Thomas K. · 233
Adknowledge, Inc. · 57, 249, 250
Adventures in Statistics · 65
Aerospace · 250
Afghanistan · 10, 123, 140, 147, 148,
149, 150, 151, 153, 154, 156, 233
  Bagram Airbase · 155, 156
  Karzai, Hamid · 148, 149, 233
Africa · 9, 119, 121, 122, 123, 125,
127, 128, 133, 158, 159, 161, 162
Aharony, Joseph · 230
Ahmadinejad, Mahmoud · 10, 129,
141, 232
Aid Trap (Hubbard and Duggan) ·
120, 124, 127
Akerlof, George · 176, 235
Allis, C. David · 237
al-Qaeda · 136, 151, 154, 233
alternative energy · 5, 21, 26, 27, 28,
29, 30, 31, 32, 33, 34, 35, 36, 37
Amazon · 51, 72, 214
American Idol · 64
Anderson, Charlie · 227
Anderson, David R. · 230
Anderson, Kaila · 231
Andrade-Cetto, Juan · 226
Android phone applications · 214
Apollo Moon Landings · 250
Apple Corporation · 169, 219
Argentina · 61
Ariely, Dan · 82, 208, 229, 236
Army · 139, 147, 150, 152, 250

Arnold, Lutz G. · 230
Arrow, Kenneth · 80
asymmetric information · 172, 176,
187
autonomy · *See* empowerment
Axe, David · 154
Ayoade, John · 236
Azuaje, Francisco · 237

B

baby boomers · 125
Baby College · 62
Baggott, Christopher · 233
Bank of America · 95, 229
banks · 95, 98, 99, 101, 110, 181, 230
banner targeting · 250
Bath Iron Works · 130
Beattie, Alan · 228
Becker, Gary · 82
behavioral economics · 71, 80, 82,
83, 209, 229
  irrationality · 7, 71, 79, 81, 82, 85,
108, 190, 208
  social relationships · 82
behavioral targeting · 51
Bendix Corporation · 250
Bernanke, Ben · 8, 98, 99, 100, 101,
110, 111, 230
Bhidé, Amar · 43, 226
bin al-Hussein, King Abdullah II ·
135, 145
Bing! · 134
*Birds on Flying: Can
Mathematical Theories Destroy
the Financial Markets?*
(Triana) · 79
birth control method · 41

birth rates · 39, 41, 124

Black Swan: The Impact of the Highly Improbable (Taleb) · 81

Blackburn, George L. · 233

Blake, John · 237

Blink (Gladwell) · 138

blogs.psychologytoday.com · 58

Bloom Energy · 34

bone density · 20, 189, 190, 193, 200, 201, 202, 203, 204, 236

bonobos · 223

boom-bust cycle · 8, 107

Booth School of Business · 250

Boreham, Paul · 232

Bosnia · 140

Boulderstone, Richard · 236

Brafman, Ori and Rom · 82, 229

brain · 13, 71, 86, 155, 157, 198, 218, 220, 221

Brant, Bob · 226

Brazil · 26, 31, 36, 63, 152, 183, 226, 235

Britain · 72, 126

Brooks, David · 22

Brooks, Rodney A. · 237

Brown, David J. · 236

Brown, Ellen · 229

Brue, Stanley L. · 237

Buffett, Warren · 87, 101, 230

Building Bone Vitality (Lanou and Castleman) · 203

C

calcium · 189, 202, 203, 235

California, University of · 77, 230

calorie restricted diet · 199

Cambridge University · 84

Camerer, Colin F. · 229

Canada · 24, 25, 26, 216

Canada, Geoffrey · 228

cancer · 12, 116, 159, 171, 179, 187, 189, 191, 192, 193, 198, 202, 218, 233, 235

capitalism · 9, 87, 88, 89, 90, 126, 127, 129, 205

carbon tax · 32, 33, 34, 37, 38, 143

Castleman, Michael · 203, 235

Catholic Church · 55, 70, 225

Catholic Diocese of Cleveland · 70

Central European University · 84

Chakraborty, D. · 234

Challenger · 22

Chance, Giles · 231

Chaplin, George · 234

Chapman, Jeff · 230

Chazin, Suzanne · 234

Chechnya · 10, 147, 149, 150, 233

Chicago, University of · 88, 111, 230, 249, 250
  Rockefeller Chapel · 88

China · 9, 18, 30, 31, 41, 43, 63, 100, 119, 120, 125, 129, 130, 131, 132, 133, 134, 151, 183, 222, 224, 231, 232

cholesterol · 19, 171, 173, 174, 192, 196, 197, 199

Cimbala, Stephen J. · 232

Clark, Arthur Hamilton · 237

Clayton, Edward T. · 233

climate · 6, 15, 22, 39, 40, 53, 54, 160, 195, 198, 227

clinical trials · *See* epidemiology:randomized trials

Clinton, William J. · 12, 196, 197

Coello, Carlos A. · 236

Cole, Michael · 227

Columbus, Christopher · 224

Communist Manifesto (Marx and Engels) · 73

comparative advantage · 43

Compare Everywhere · 214

compound interest formula · 181

Congo River Basin · 223

Congress · 5, 23, 31, 32, 34, 36, 101, 110, 117, 132, 178, 180, 185
contagion effects · 79, 111
Cowles Foundation · 229
Craigslist · 49
C-reactive protein · 19
Creative Capitalism (Kinsley) · 87
Crowley, James · 11, 162
crude oil · 5, 15, 21, 26, 28, 29, 31, 32, 37
currency · 19, 93, 94, 95, 96, 97, 120, 121, 122, 143, 145
cytokine-10 · 202, 204
cytokine-6 · 202, 204
Czech Republic · 142

D

DailyMe.com · 52
Dancing with the Stars · 64
Darwin, Charles · 10, 91, 92, 158, 160, 229, 233
Davenport, Thomas H. · 228
Davos, Switzerland · 87
Dawkins, Marvin P. · 233
De Santis, Corrado · 236
Dead Aid (Moyo) · 119, 121, 231
Del Cogliano, Davide · 236
Dell Computer's Design Studio · 73
Demin, A. V. · 237
Deming, Edwards · 120
Denmark · 26, 31
Dhaenens, Clarisse · 236
Dickens, Charles · 135, 232
DNA · 13, 20, 160, 187, 211, 212, 222
Doble, Rick · 236
Dobson, Thomas · 229, 231
Doing Business (World Bank) · 124, 231
Dong, Zhao Yang · 227
Douglas, Ronald G. · 233
Drew, Elizabeth · 234

driving while texting (DWT) · 11, 164, 165
Dubner, Stephen J. · 228
Duggan, William · 120, 124, 126, 231
Dukkipati, Rao V. · 233
Dutch disease · 122, 143

E

E Ink Corporation · 214
E85 · 26, 35, 36
Earth Resources Technology Satellite · 250
e-Bay · 72
Ebenstein, Lanny · 228
ebooks · 68
econometrics · 105, 106, 109, 249
    artificial neural networks · 218
    asymptotic analysis · 114
    Bayesian models · 42, 226
    collaborative filter · 51, 52, 134
    decision tree models · 42
    interaction effects · 116, 117
    lagged variables · 112, 113
    neural network algorithm · 46
    nonparametric models · 114
    state space models · 42
    stepwise regression · 114
Economic Cooperation Administration (ECA) · 127
Economic Policy Institute · 230
Eddy, David M. · 235
education · 6, 16, 34, 47, 55, 60, 61, 62, 63, 66, 75, 106, 133, 135, 144, 145, 182, 184
    students · 6, 51, 55, 60, 61, 62, 63, 64, 65, 66, 67, 77, 81, 85, 86, 104, 112, 136, 153, 160, 208, 249
    video games · 7, 16, 55, 63, 65, 66
efficient market theory · 84, 87, 88, 110

Einstein, Albert · 57, 59, 219, 225
Eisenhower, Dwight D. · 177
Ekbom, Anders · 235
Eldridge, Erik B. · 233
Elias, Stephen · 234
Ely, Richard T. · 235
Emerson, Ralph Waldo · 90
empowerment · 18, 61, 62
End of History and the Last Man
    (Fukuyama) · 73, 228
energy independence · 5, 21, 24, 25,
    26
energy markets · 21
Engels, Friederich · 73, 228
epidemiology · 105, 106
    epigenetics · 223
    randomized trials · 115, 116, 117
        control group · 115
        double blind · 115
        placebo · 115
        treatment group · 115, 116, 147,
            163, 175, 186, 187
Eskimos · 160
Espresso Book Machine · 7, 68, 228
ethanol · 26, 30, 34, 35, 36, 226
Euro Zone · 96
European Union · 41, 97, 128, 142
Evolution of Species (Darwin) · 91
external freedom · 19, 120, 129

Filipe, Joaquin · 226
financial derivatives · 46, 85, 89
financial system · 16, 94, 99
Financial Times · 49, 226
fiscal policy · 77, 81, 102
fixed costs · 44, 45, 88, 168
Flynn Effect · 6, 56, 57, 58, 59, 227
Flynn, James R. · 56, 227
Food and Drug Administration ·
    115, 116, 117, 174
Ford Motor Company · 194, 217
forecasting · 8, 9, 105, 106, 108, 109,
    112, 113, 114
foreign aid · 9, 119, 121, 122, 123,
    124
Fort Hood · 136, 139, 140, 232
Fort Knox · 67, 194
Fort Leavenworth · 147, 151
France · 26, 31, 126, 226
Francis, Keith A. · 229
Frank, Robert H. · 230, 234
Free Agent Nation (Pink) · 71, 73
free enterprise · 16, 17, 65, 125, 176
Free Market Madness (Ubel) · 82
Friedman, Milton · 77, 108, 111,
    228, 230
Friedman, Thomas · 232
Fukuyama, Francis · 73, 228
Furuichi, Takeshi · 237

F

Facebook · 45, 49, 168, 213, 224
Fair Isaac · 49
Federal Deposit Insurance
    Corporation · 93
Federal Express (FedEx) · 183
Federal Reserve Bank · 93, 94, 99,
    108, 110, 111
Ferguson, Cassandra · 236
Ferguson, James M. · 236
Ferguson, Niall · 232
Ferrier, Jean-Louis · 226

G

Galbraith, John Kenneth · 48, 227
Galilei, Galileo · 59, 219, 225
Gallagher, J. Chris · 236
game theory · 80
Gardner, Harold H. · 235
gasoline · 5, 15, 21, 30, 31, 33, 34, 35,
    36, 37, 38
Gates, Bill · 7, 87, 89, 90
Gates, Henry Louis Jr. · 11, 162,
    234
Geanakopolos, John · 229

Geithner, Tim · 8, 98, 99, 100, 101, 230
Gelman, Andrew · 226
General Motors · 45, 217
Germany · 31
Giffen good · 81
Gillespie, James R. · 237
Gladwell, Malcolm · 138, 187, 232, 235
Glielmo, Luigi · 236
global warming · *See* climate
Go, Vay Liang W. · 233
Gonzalez, Roberto J. · 233
Google · 6, 52, 56, 60, 62, 68, 134, 212, 218, 237
Google Books · 62
Gosling, F. G. · 237
Gouwens, Judith A. · 235
Governing the Commons (Ostrom) · 78
Gowan, Jackie · 232
GPS locator · 154, 215, 224
Great Tea Race of 1866 · 224
Greece · 96, 97
green jobs · 5, 26, 31, 34, 35
Greene, William H. · 230
Greenemeier, Larry · 234
Gridlock Economy (Heller) · 78
Griswold, William G. · 234
gross domestic product · 61, 119, 144
Gross, Myron D. · 235
Grossman, Michael · 235
Grunwald, Michael · 230
Gubser, Steven S. · 237
Gulf of Mexico · 22

H

Hagstrom, Robert G. · 230
Haiti · 123, 231
Hall, Robert · 232
Halvorson, George · 235

Handoyo, Stefan S. · 226
Harlem · 62, 228
Harper, Frederick D. · 233
Harris, Jeanne G. · 228
Harrison, John · 34
Harvard Book Store · 68
Harvard University · 11, 38, 51, 68, 75, 80, 162, 228, 229
    Widener Library · 68
Hasan, Nidal Malik · 10, 136, 139, 140
Hastings, Reed · 52
Hatch, Nathan · 70
Hauser, Eduardo · 52
Hawkes Learning Systems · 64, 65
Hawkes, James J. · 228
Hawkes, James S. · 228
health care · 11, 16, 171, 172, 175, 176, 177, 178, 179, 180, 184, 185, 186, 209, 234
    health insurance · 11, 103, 171, 172, 177, 178, 180, 181, 182, 183, 185, 204
health strategy · 62, 193, 196
heart attack · 116, 171, 173, 174, 195, 199
Heart Revolution: the extraordinary discovery that finally laid the cholesterol myth to rest (McCully) · 197
Heber, David · 233
Heffetz, Ori · 234
Heij, C. · 233
Heller, Michael · 78, 228
Hemenway, David · 234
Henriksen, K. · 236
Henze, Rosemary C. · 234
heterodox economics · 77
Heufer, Jan · 228
Hickmann, Meredith A. · 230
Hidden Persuaders (Packard) · 48
Hirsch, Fred · 80, 229
Hoey, Dennis · 232
Holder, Benjamin · 232

Holder, Charles F. · 233
Holick, Michael F. · 233
Hollander, Samuel · 229
Hollywood · 72, 137, 219
homocysteine · 19, 196, 197, 198
Honorary Degree Committee · 70
housing market · 79, 85, 207, 216
Howard-Johnson, Carolyn · 236
Hubbard, Glenn · 120, 124, 126, 231
human capital · 76, 123
human terrain system · 148, 153
Humayoon, Haseeb · 233
Hurrell, James W. · 227

I

immigration · 39, 41, 42
Impossibility Theorem (Arrow) · 80
In Defense of Food (Pollan) · 203
incentives · 10, 16, 23, 55, 63, 65, 66,
    101, 157, 171, 175, 185, 189, 209
    fee-for-service · 11, 16, 185, 205
Indiana University · 77
*Inquiry into the Nature and
    Causes of the Wealth of Nations*
    (Smith) · 80, 91, 207
Institute for New Economic
    Thinking · 84
interdependence · 18, 21, 22, 79, 80
interest rates · 93, 99, 100, 102, 107,
    108, 109, 112
internal freedom · 19, 120, 129, 131
Internal Revenue Service · 94
international park system · 217
International Space Station · 217
Internet · 45, 47, 56, 57, 61, 62, 63,
    68, 71, 72, 86, 121, 168, 188, 211,
    215, 221, 225, 250
Intille, Stephen S. · 234
Investors Business Daily · 49
Ip, Kwan Fun · 227
IQ scores · 6, 56, 57, 59

Iran · 9, 29, 30, 121, 122, 135, 141,
    142, 151, 226, 231, 232
Iraq · 10, 140, 145, 151, 153
Iron Law of Population (Malthus)
    · 92
irrational · *See* behavioral
    economics:irrationality
Isidore, Chris · 230
Israel · 9, 29, 31, 135, 141, 144, 232

J

Jablonski, Nina · 160, 234
Jaccard, James · 231
Jacobson, Sheldon H. · 234
Japan · 18, 37, 41, 120, 129, 216
Jenuwein, Thomas · 237
Jiangdu Yuchai Shipbuilding
    Company · 130
Jourdan, Laetitia · 236
Journal of Business · 230
journalism · 40, 249

K

Kansas, University of · 117, 231
Kaplan, Siena · 227
Karabell, Zachary · 232
Karris, Steven T. · 230
Kaufman, Scott Barry · 58, 227
Kennedy, Edward · 198
Key2SafeDriving · 164
Keynes, John Maynard · 77, 81, 228
Kibbe, Mathew B. · 230
King, Martin Luther Jr. · 161, 162
Kinsley, Michael · 87, 229
Kiva.org · 9, 121, 127, 128, 231
Klein, Natalie · 237
Korea · 130
Korosec, Kirsten · 226
Kosovo · 140

L

labor markets · 42, 43, 44, 71, 76, 86, 87, 96, 103, 104, 124, 133, 204, 205, 230
Lanou, Amy Joy · 203, 235
Launius, Roger · 231
Lazzaro, Joseph · 232
Leal, Kendra Mae · 237
Leitman, Seth · 226
Levin, G. G. · 237
Levine, Michael · 37, 38, 226
Levitin, Karl · 227
Levitt, Steven D. · 228, 234
Levy, Michael · 226
Li, Xue · 227
Liebman, Bonnie · 236
lights out manufacturing · 133
Lincoln, Abraham · 161
LinkedIn · 213
Linux · 23
Lo, Andrew · 89, 229
Loewenstein, George · 229
Logsdon, John · 231
Long Term Capital Management · 81
low-acid eating · 20, 189, 193, 204
Lucas, Paul · 226
Luria, Alexander · 58, 227
Lyles, Alan · 236
Lynch, Wendy D. · 235
Lynn, Scott · 57, 249

M

MacKinlay, Craig · 89, 229
Maes, Pattie · 237
Mahtafar, Tara · 232
Malkiel, Burton G. · 230
malpractice lawsuits · 175, 185, 206, 207
Malthus, Thomas · 92, 229

Mankiw, N. Gregory · 228
Maraniss, David · 231
marginal cost · 49
market failure · 17, 32, 74, 176, 177, 186, 209
marketing · 40, 42, 71, 227
Marketing Science · 250
Mars · 13, 110, 216, 225, 230
Marsh, Jan · 162, 249
Marsh, Jeff · 69
Marsh, William H. · 228
Marshall plan · 126, 127
Martin, Grant · 154
Martin, Gus · 232
Marx, Karl · 16, 73, 228
    Communist Manifesto · 73
    Marxism · 63
Maslin, Jamie · 232
Massachusetts Institute of Technology · 51, 113, 214, 237
Matthews, John N.S. · 231
Mayersohn, Jeffrey · 68
Mays, Elizabeth · 227
McBrewster, John · 232
McConnell, Campbell R. · 237
McCully, Kilmer S. · 197
McDonalds · 69
McFate, Montgomery · 154
McGlynn, Maureen · 234
McKay, David · 227
McNamara, Robert · 153, 156
McNutt, Patrick A. · 234
Medicare · 39, 42, 181, 182, 219
Medvedev, Dmitry · 142, 143
mental energy · 7, 56, 58, 63, 67, 71, 83, 85, 86, 87, 103, 157, 211
Merrigan, Court · 228
Mexico · 22, 24, 25, 27
Michels, Karin B. · 235
Microsoft Corporation · 169, 219
Middle East · 9, 135, 139, 140, 145
Midwest Econometrics Group · 250
Miller, Frederic · 232
Miller, Michael · 237

Millwood, Nancy Huehnergarth · 235

Milner, John · 233

Mind of the Market (Shermer) · 91

Minsky, Hyman P. · 228

Mirowski, Philip · 76, 228

MIT Media Lab · 214

monetary policy · 23, 65, 77, 81, 82, 83, 95, 96, 102, 111, 133

money · 13, 38, 116, 130, 181, 196, 205, 214

moral hazard · 172, 178, 179, 221

More Heat than Light (Mirowski) · 76

Moreira, Lino · 235

Morgan, Stephen L. · 231

Morrison, Wayne M. · 231

Moses, Yolanda T. · 234

Moyo, Dambisa · 119, 121, 122, 123, 231

Mukhopadhyay, Carol Chapnick · 234

Murphy, Paul · 233

MySpace · 45

N

NAACP · 159

Nance, Malcolm · 233

nanobots · 224

nanosurgery · 13, 218, 225

nanotechnology · 13, 20, 211, 212, 218, 225

National Geographic · 223

national park system · 217

national security · 23, 24, 25, 26, 28, 29, 33, 156

natural gas · 26, 122, 143, 145

natural resource curse · *See* Dutch disease

Natural Theology (Paley) · 91

Neboshynsky, Andrew J. · 233

negative externalities · 17, 32, 33, 209, 221

Nellis Air Force Base · 155

Netanyahu, Benjamin · 10, 135, 144, 145, 232

Netflix · 23, 52, 65, 184

New York Times · 49, 226, 235

New York University School of Law · 38

Newfarmer, Richard S. · 235

newspapers · 6, 39, 40, 48, 49, 51, 52, 53, 162, 163, 250

Nikolaev, Alexander G. · 234

Nixon, Richard · 162, 234

Nobel Prize · 7, 39, 43, 51, 77, 79, 80, 82, 126, 176, 187

No-Eat-Day Diet · 12, 189, 190, 191

non-governmental aid organizations (NGOs) · 126

Nonrandom Walk Down Wall Street (Lo and MacKinlay) · 89

Northwest Flight 253 · 136, 137

Notre Dame, University of · 7, 55, 64, 69, 70, 228, 249, 250

Novaya Zemiya · 58

Nudge (Sunstein and Thaler) · 187

O

O'Neill, Ian · 230

Obama, Barack · 7, 9, 10, 11, 22, 26, 69, 70, 120, 131, 132, 133, 134, 135, 140, 142, 143, 149, 151, 153, 174, 185

Ogletree, Charles · 234

Ohsawa, Yukio · 227

oil · *See* crude oil

On Demand Books · 68

OPEC · 24, 25, 30

osteoporosis · 12, 20, 189, 193, 200, 201, 203, 236

Ostrom, Elinor · 77, 82, 228

P

Packard, Vance · 48, 227
Page, Larry · 212
Pakistan · 128, 140, 150, 151, 154
Paley, William · 91, 92, 229
Pallin, Carolina Vendil · 233
Paradox of Choice (Schwartz) · 82
Pareto optimality · 89
Parker, Rachel · 232
Parry, Dave · 236
partially hydrogenated · 19, 197
Patrick, Kevin · 234
Patterson, Scott · 227
Pennsylvania State University · 160
Pepper, Miriam · 249
Persian Gulf · 142
Petraeus, David · 153
petro-dictatorships · 25, 143, 145
Petruno, Tom · 229
Philbin, Tom · 236
Phillips, David · 226
Pink, Daniel H. · 71, 73, 228
Poland · 142
Polk, William R. · 231
Pollan, Michael · 203, 236
pollution · 17, 32, 33, 74, 77, 209
Popat, Ketul · 237
Port-au-Prince · 123
Porter, Jack · 234
Portland Press Herald · 232
positive externalities · 17, 32
Posner, Richard A. · 226
Potter, Harry · 47, 216
Predictably Irrational (Ariely) · 82, 208
price floor · 5, 15, 21, 26, 28, 29, 30, 31, 32, 34, 35, 36, 37
   self-adjusting · 15, 34, 35, 36, 37
Principles Of Scientific Management (Taylor) · 205
prostate cancer · 159

Public Broadcasting Service (PBS) · 144, 232
Putin, Vladimir · 142, 143, 216

Q

Quant Systems · 228
Quint, Thomas · 229

R

Raab, Fred · 234
Rabin, Mathew · 229
Rabin, Roni Caryn · 235
Radzicki, Michael Joseph · 230
Rahn, Pete · 165
Ray, P. K. · 237
real wages · 42
recalcitrant patient problem · 177
Reichrath, Jörg · 233
Reinberg, Danny · 237
relational databases · 218
revealed preference · 51, 52, 76
Riccardo, David · 124, 231
Ripley, Brian D. · 237
Robbins, Matthew J. · 234
Robinson-Patman Act · 226
Rockefeller, John D. · 27
Roe, Mark · 37, 38, 226
Rolfes, Sharon Rady · 236
Rose, Charlie · 144, 232
Rosner, Bernard · 231
Rosser, John Barkley · 233
Rubens, David · 232
Russia · 27, 29, 30, 41, 43, 126, 130, 142, 143, 145, 147, 149, 150, 169, 181, 216, 217, 225, 232, 233
Ruvinsky, Anatoly · 237

S

Saint Anselm College · 232
Samuelson, Paul · 7, 51, 75, 77, 227
Sanders, Hugh B. · 235
Santa Fe Institute · 84, 112
Sargent, Rob · 227
SAT scores · 6, 56, 57
Saudi Arabia · 29, 30
School of Advanced Military
    Studies (SAMS) · 151, 152, 153
Schwartz, Barry · 82, 229
Schwarzenegger, Arnold · 95
Segaran, Toby · 227
Selengut, Charles · 232
Shakespeare, William · 57
Shermer, Michael · 91, 229
Sherwood, Lauralee · 237
Shop Savvy · 214
Shubik, Martin · 229
Smith, Adam · 80, 91, 92, 124, 207
Smith, H.C. · 230
Smith, Robert · 231
Smoke, Clinton H. · 235
Sobel, Dava · 226
Social Limits to Growth (Hirsch) ·
    80
Social Security · 39, 42, 182
socialism · 8, 11, 89, 90, 92, 124, 125,
    126, 127, 172, 182, 183, 184, 235
Soong, Seng-jaw · 117, 231
Sorensen, George · 232
Sorkin, Andrew Ross · 226
Soros, George · 84
South Bend, Indiana · 162
Soviet Union · 27, 58, 73, 125, 231
Spence, Michael · 176
sputnik (satellite) · 125
Starbucks · 69
statistical design strategist · 250
statistician, definition of · 181
Statistics in Medicine · 250
Status Seekers (Packard) · 48
stem cells · 20

Stiglitz, Joseph · 176
Stim, Richard · 234
Subconscious Diet (Sanders) · 235
subconscious mind · 12, 67, 140,
    193, 194, 196
subsidies · 16, 17, 123
Sudoku · 65
sugar cane · 26
Sunstein, Cass · 187, 235
super-private good · 167
super-public good · 168
Swary, Itzhak · 230
Sway (Brafman and Brafman) · 82
Sweeny, Dennis J. · 230
Symonds, Judith · 236
system dynamics · 8, 9, 84, 105, 106,
    109, 112, 113, 114
    feedback loops · 64, 88, 108, 113,
        124, 151, 152
    system dynamics software · 114

T

Tale of Two Cities (Dickens) · 135
Taleb, Nassim · 81, 229
Taliban · 147, 150, 154
Tanne, Janice Hopkins · 232
tariff · 5, 21, 27, 28, 29, 30, 31, 37, 38,
    120, 132, 226
taxes · 11, 16, 21, 38, 93, 94, 97, 98,
    101, 171, 178, 180, 209, 219, 235
Taylor, Frederick W. · 205
Taylorism · 205
Technischen Universität
    Dortmund · 228
terrorists · 9, 28, 136, 137, 161, 189
Tesla Motors · 45
Thailand · 131
Thaler, Richard · 187, 235
Thompson, Jo · 237
Thompson, Paul · 232
Three Mile Island · 22
Time Magazine · 98, 101, 230

Timmins, Graham · 232
Tipping Point (Gladwell) · 187
Togo · 128
Tough, Paul · 228
traditional economics · 71, 79, 81, 82, 83, 84, 113, 207
transfats · 19, 197, 198
Treasury Department · 99
Trebat, Thomas J. · 235
Triana, Pablo · 79, 229
Tsuruoka, Sonia · 228
Turner, John Roscoe · 232
Turrisi, Robert · 231
Twitter · 45

U

U.N. Convention on the Law of the Sea · 217
Ubel, Peter · 82, 229
Uganda · 41
undersea farms · 217
unemployment · 72, 95, 96, 101, 152
United Nations · 22, 144, 156, 212, 216, 237
United Parcel Service (UPS) · 183
University College London · 136

V

Van Loon, Harry · 227
Vandome, Agnes · 232
Venezuela · 29, 30, 122, 145
Venturesome Economy (Bhidé) · 43, 226
VeraSun Energy · 27
Vietnam · 10, 120, 133, 147, 149, 150, 151, 154, 156, 250
Village Books, Bellingham, WA · 68
vitamin D · 160, 202, 233, 235
volatility · 15, 19, 21, 26

W

Wagner, Christian · 227
Wald, Matthew L. · 226
Wall Street Journal · 49
Wal-Mart · 13, 36, 120, 132, 211, 213
Wang, Shuliang · 227
Washington, George · 161
wealth strategy · 62, 196
Weindruch, Richard · 235
Wells, Karin Lynn · 228
Wendy's · 162
Whitman, Glen · 236
Whitney, Eleanor Noss · 236
Whyte, Lancelot Law · 235
Widener Library · *See* Harvard University
Wikipedia · 23, 56, 134, 230
Williams, Thomas A. · 230
Williamson, Oliver · 77, 82, 228
wind power · 25, 26, 34, 123, 226
Winship, Christopher · 231
wizards of the 21st century · 47
Wong, Stanley · 227
World Bank · 69, 124, 231
    Info Shop · 69
World Economic Forum · 87
World Trade Organization · 30, 132, 142, 143
World War II · 120, 125, 126, 129
Wright brothers · 110
Wu, Hulin · 230

Y

Yada, Katsutoshi · 227

Z

Zellen, Bary Scott · 237
Zhang, Jin-Ting · 230

Acknowledgements

I am grateful to my friends and colleagues from the University of Notre Dame and the University of Chicago for their insights and arguments both for and against the various analyses and policy proposals presented in this book. I am particularly grateful to my former graduate students who made many suggestions for improvements and shared my objective of trying to get people to think more carefully about the issues they cared the most about.

Similarly, I would like to thank the journalists from the South Bend Tribune and the Kansas City Star who taught me and showed me excellence in journalism. I am especially grateful to Miriam Pepper and Yael Abouhalkah. I have learned that there is always room for improvement the next day on the next story or the next column. People who just try to do their best are often discouraged, but people who seek perfection are never discouraged. They know they can never reach their goal, but they always keep trying anyway.

Many of my former classmates and some of my dearest relatives played a key role in keeping me on track and helping me maintain my sense of humor (or humour in the case of my British cousins). I was often outgunned by their superior intellect and had to make appropriate adjustments to my commentary accordingly.

My colleagues at Adknowledge, Inc. were particularly helpful in stimulating my imagination on one hand, and forcing me to face reality on the other. My experience there reinforced my long held belief that the most powerful people are those who have both the vision to see new opportunities and the technical know-how to exploit those opportunities in a timely and effective manner. Problems can be analyzed to death, but at the end of the day solutions must found that actually work. I learned a great deal from the dynamic leadership of Adknowledge's CEO Scott Lynn.

Most of all I am grateful to my wife, Jan, who gave up her position as Assistant Managing Editor of the South Bend Tribune to follow me to Kansas City and, ultimately, use her editorial skills to help me transform from a numbers guy (econometrics) to a word guy (writing columns). We share a great respect for the power of the written word and the publish-or-perish mandate.

About the Author

Lawrence C. Marsh is concurrently professor emeritus in the Department of Economics at the University of Notre Dame and visiting professor of econometrics and statistics in the MBA program at the University of Chicago's Booth School of Business in Autumn 2010.

He taught graduate and undergraduate economics at Notre Dame for 30 years. He served as Director of Notre Dame's Ph.D. program in economics for 13 years. He has also worked in business operations and management in the Aerospace Industry and for an Internet advertising and online auction company. He studied the Coal Industry underground in longwall and continuous mining operations. He contributes to the Kansas City Star online edition as an independent Midwest Voices columnist.

After serving in the U.S. Army in Vietnam, he returned home to take a job with Bendix Corporation's Aerospace Division as subcontract administrator and contract personnel administrator on the Apollo Moon Landings Mission, the Earth Resources Technology Satellite and a number of classified military projects. He co-created the Midwest Econometrics Group, which he directed for 15 years. More recently, he worked at the Internet advertising company *Adknowledge, Inc.* where he served as the head of analytics for banner targeting and as "statistical design strategist" in devising algorithms that send billions of banner ads to websites all over the Internet. He has contributed to hundreds of publications including articles in the *Journal of Econometrics, Marketing Science, Statistics in Medicine* and many other professional journals as well as numerous newspaper columns, book chapters and books.

In teaching he won the James A. Burns award for excellence in graduate teaching in 1990-91 and was an O'Malley Award Nominee for undergraduate teaching in 1995-96. In 2002-2003 he was selected as a Kaneb Faculty Teaching Fellow for excellence in teaching. He has served on a large number of Ph.D. dissertation committees and has given several thousand lectures in graduate and undergraduate statistics, econometrics, mathematical economics and microeconomic theory. In quasi-retirement he spends his time writing and editing a variety of articles, books and newspaper columns.

Made in the USA
Monee, IL
28 August 2021